Mulled Words

for Barbara
Happy mulling !

Marjorie

AWE BREAD CHRIST
DESIRE EARTH FREE GROW

Mulled Words

A Word a Week from God's Word

HOPE INTEGRITY JOY KEEP
LOVE MAKE NEW OVERCOME
PRAYER QUIET RECEIVE SHINE
TRUST UNDERSTAND VOICE
WORK EXALT YOUNG ZEAL

Marjorie Gray

Pleasant Word
A Division of WINEPRESS PUBLISHING

Pleasant Word (a division of WinePress Publishing, PO Box 428, Enumclaw, WA 98022) functions only as book publisher. As such, the ultimate design, content, editorial accuracy, and views expressed or implied in this work are those of the author.

Unless otherwise noted, all Scriptures are taken from the *Holy Bible, Today's New International Version*™ *TNIV*®. Copyright © 2001, 2005 by International Bible Society. All rights reserved worldwide.

Other Scripture versions cited:
AB – *Amplified Bible* © 1965 by Zondervan Publishing House.
JB – *Jerusalem Bible* © 1968 by Doubleday & Company.
KJV – *King James Version* in Eight Translation New Testament
   © 1974 by The Iverson-Norman Associates.
LB – *Living Bible* © 1971 by Tyndale House Publishers.
MSG – *THE MESSAGE* © 2002 by Eugene H. Peterson.
   Used by permission of NavPress Publishing Group.
NEB – *New English Bible* © 1970 by Oxford University Press and Cambridge University Press.
NIV – *New International Bible NIV Study Bible*
   © 1985 by The Zondervan Corporation.
NKJV – *New King James Version* © 1982 by Thomas Nelson, Inc.
Phillips – *The New Testament in Modern English* by J. B. Phillips
   © 1957 The Macmillan Company.
RSV – *Revised Standard Version* © 1971 by Thomas Nelson & Sons.

Poem "Crucifixion" on page 16:
   Thomas John Carlisle, *Looking for Jesus* ©1993
   Wm. B. Eerdmans Publishing Company, Grand Rapids, Michigan.
   Reprinted by permission of the publisher; all rights reserved.

ISBN 13: 978-1-4141-1247-3
ISBN 10: 1-4141-1247-5
Library of Congress Catalog Card Number: 2008904370

Contents

Pronouns for God

As is customary in *Today's New International Version* and most of the other Scripture versions cited, I do not capitalize pronouns referring to the deity in these devotionals. However, as is my custom in addressing God in my journal, I do capitalize such pronouns in the prayers concluding each devotional.

Acknowledgements

I would like to express my appreciation for much assistance in mulling these words. From the very beginning my mother, Clarice Ribbens, read each series of seven, prayed with me about them, and encouraged me greatly. In the end many friends each read one series of seven, and most of them graciously gave suggestions for improvement which I gladly incorporated. They are as follows: Cheryl Hellner, Dave and Joyce Campbell, Paula Vander Hoven, Helen Den Boer, Patrick Jasperse, Jim Gray, Rod Jellema, Jean Roorda, Al Chase, Lori Martin, Jenise Williamson, Anne Marie Gabriele, Morris Ledbetter, Tom Gardner, and various members of the Greenbelt Writers' Group.

—Marjorie Gray

Awestruck

Read Genesis 28:10-22.

> **"How awesome is this place! This is none other than the house of God; this is the gate of heaven."**
> **—Genesis 28:17**

AWE IN THE Bible combines fear, wonder and reverence in response to God. Why did Jacob's dream fill him with awe? It was not a nightmare but a glorious vision of a stairway linking earth and heaven with "angels of God" going up and down. From the top God identified himself and renewed the promises he had made to Jacob's father and grandfather. The dreamscape was awesome; the angels were awesome; the promises of land and protection were awesome. Most awesome of all was God's revelation of himself by his voice and by his foretelling: "All peoples on earth will be blessed through you and your offspring" (14).

When Jacob woke up the vision and voice were gone. But Jacob was in awe, realizing that God had opened "the gate of heaven" to him. He set up the stone he had used for a pillow as a memorial to which he could return when his faith needed renewing.

Like Jacob, we mark places and times where we have been awestruck. Sometimes our markers commemorate disaster and death, such as at places like Ground Zero or highway guardrails. Yet even in the most unlikely places, as well as in churches, we stand in awe as we begin to understand Jesus' claim: "I am the gate; whoever enters through me will be saved" (John 10:9).

Strike us with awe as You open heaven's door to us, O Lord, by Your Word and Spirit.

The Awesome One

Read Deuteronomy 10:12-22.

> "For the Lord your God is God of gods and Lord of lords, the great God, mighty and awesome...."
>
> —Deuteronomy 10:17

LIKE THE ISRAELITES, churches and Christians today may be led through wilderness passages. God has delivered us from the life-destroying forces which were dominating us. He has blessed us with leaders. He has given us his law, a comprehensive guide to right and good living. But life is still hard, maybe harder and more bewildering than before. What can we do to stay on track?

God is not merely our personal "higher power" but the highest power, the awe-inspiring holy one, the supreme being who is absolutely autonomous. Moses commands the people to fear God (12 and 20). Only a proper respect for the infinite creator enables us to see ourselves realistically as finite creatures. We are made for awe and worship. As Moses says, "He is your praise" (21).

The mighty, awesome God can never be manipulated, nor can we boast that he is ours alone, but God is personal. Moses tells the Israelites: "he is your God, who performed for you those great and awesome wonders you saw with your own eyes" (21). He is our God today, because of Jesus and the Holy Spirit.

Move us to awe before You, Lord God Almighty. Forgive our ignoring of You and taking You for granted.

Awed by the Book

"My flesh trembles in fear of you; I stand in awe of your laws."

—Psalm 119:120

PSALM 119 IS a 176-verse meditation on the wonders of God's Word. The unnamed psalmist testifies to God's people; he praises, petitions and makes vows to God, focusing on holy Scripture in each verse. Laws, statutes, ways, precepts, decrees, commandments and promises are other names he uses for God's Word. The psalmist expresses a full gamut of emotion—from goose bumps, quivers or shivers, to shame and unworthiness, viewing Scripture as he views God.

According to a dictionary of idioms, the phrase "stand in awe of" originally meant to "fear something or someone." Gradually this changed to "dread mingled with respect" and then "reverence."

How do we approach God's Word? Can we cultivate awe? Standing in awe is standing at attention. In some churches the congregation stands to hear the gospel reading. Paying attention to the Bible at home each day can be reinforced by reading passages and devotionals aloud to each other. Sharing awe-inspiring insights and times of prayer and praise are other ways to respond to holy Scripture.

Almighty God, forgive our glib entrances into Your holy presence and casual skimming of Your Word. May Your Spirit rekindle our awe and empower us to obey You.

Everyday Awe

"I stand in awe of your deeds, Lord. Renew them in our day, in our time make them known; in wrath remember mercy."
—Habakkuk 3:2

GOD IS HUGE, far more powerful than we can imagine. Yet the centuries-old human tendency is to ignore or at least minimize God. Many believe in God as the creator or prime mover; some say God did miracles "in Bible times," and some affirm that God still works "behind the scenes" throughout history. Some insurance policies still refer to natural disasters as "acts of God."

Habakkuk's prayer moves us to prayerful awe. We reach out to God even in our fear and shock at the devastations of earthquakes, hurricanes, pandemics, terrorist attacks, war and persecution. We plead with God on behalf of his people everywhere in our day, in our time.

God's power thunders and roars in awful storms, but more regularly shines in the beauties of raindrops and snowflakes, dew and frost, sunrise and sunset, moon, planets and stars. Though awful human powers wreak havoc, God rules not in wrath, but in the grace and mercy of Jesus Christ, the Lord of lords. What a relief to realize that God's love is far more powerful and evident than his anger.

Forgive us for blaming You in times of tragedy, Father. Open our eyes to Your constant love.

Global Awe

Read Zephaniah 2:1-11.

> **"The Lord will be awesome to them when he destroys all the gods of the earth. Distant nations will bow down to him, all of them in their own lands."**
>
> —Zephaniah 2:11

THE PROPHET ZEPHANIAH begins this chapter with a message of judgment and a call to humble repentance for Judah. Most of the prophets actually warn God's covenant people, Israel and Judah, far more than nations where God is not known.

Christians, like God's Old Testament people, profess to worship the one true God. We cheer God's destruction of idols and idol-worshipers, eagerly anticipating the day when "every knee will bow" to Christ the Lord. However, our belligerent, know-it-all attitude may blind us to our own idolatry.

Will the forces of nature be unleashed by an "act of God" in volcano or flood causing the collapse of "temples" such as malls, stadiums, and corporate, military, government or religious edifices? Will God expose the true extent of our idol worship by allowing civilization to destroy itself due to global warming or nuclear annihilation?

Whenever and whatever happens, God the destroyer will be far more awesome than the destruction he causes. God will be awesome to all people everywhere.

Holy God, may we worship you alone. Come soon, Lord Jesus; may Your truth, power and love be awesome to all.

In Awe of the Godman

Read Luke 7:11-17.

> **"They were all filled with awe and praised God."**
>
> —Luke 7:16a

WE VALIDATE AND measure the success of political candidates or spiritual gurus by the crowds they attract. In the Gospels we often read of large crowds gathering around Jesus. He was famous for teaching with "authority" (see Luke 4:32) and for awesome miracles, especially healings.

But now Jesus goes beyond healing in raising a dead person to life. Some in the crowd may know about Elijah raising the son of the widow of Zarephath and Elisha bringing the Shunammite woman's son back to life. But seeing the dead son of the widow right there in Nain sit up in response to Jesus' command and hearing the now live young man's voice is incredibly awesome, even shocking.

People begin to realize that Jesus not only has supernatural powers, but personally represents God. From our perspective, three awe-compelling revelations occur. First Jesus lives out God's love: his heart goes out to the grieving widow; he says, "Don't cry," and he touches the bier, ignoring rules about possible contact with corpses (13, 14). Next Jesus speaks God's powerful word of life: "Young man, I say to you, get up!" (14). Finally Jesus moves many to praise God: "God has come to help his people," they say, and the news spreads all around (16 and 17).

Lord Jesus, we praise You for Your powerful, loving gift of life.

Awe-filled Worship

Read Hebrews 12:18-28.

> "…worship God acceptably with reverence and awe…."
> —Hebrews 12:28

ANCIENT PEOPLE WERE in awe of the four elements—earth, air, fire and water. In Scripture God inspired writers to visualize him at different times as an awesome rock, breath or wind, pillar of cloud or fire, river or fountain. Today people still stand in awe at the sight of wonders of nature like Niagara Falls or The Grand Canyon.

Thank God he not only affirms his majesty in creation, but walks and talks with human beings, as he did with our first parents, Adam and Eve. Thank God that when we turn away from him, he calls us back to covenant agreement. God is totally awesome. God cannot be appeased or accessed on our own initiative. Trying to gain God's favor by keeping rules or performing sacred rituals is like playing with fire.

To know God is to be in awe of him because of Jesus. Worshiping God is the awe of humble wonder. The covenant has changed. Zion, the "Mountain of Joy" has replaced Sinai, "the Mountain of Fear" (TNIV section title). But God is still a consuming fire—"torching all that needs to burn, getting rid of all the religious junk so that the unshakable essentials stand clear and uncluttered" (27, 28 MSG).

Holy, awesome One, You are God. May we worship You in the Spirit and in truth (John 4:24). May we never make light of Your passionate love in Jesus. May Your words shake us to awed attention.

Bread for the Journey

Read 1 Kings 19

> "He looked around and there by his head was some bread, baked over hot coals and a jar of water."
>
> —1 Kings 19:6

BREAD IS NOT only the staff of life, a basic staple, and along with water the standard survival ration, it is also comfort food. Of all the bread stories in the Bible, my favorite is Elijah's bread and water meal served by "the angel of the Lord" (7). The prophet feared for his life after Queen Jezebel swore to have him killed. How quickly he forgot God's spectacular answer to his prayers for rain on Mount Carmel! Did he also forget how "the power of the Lord came on" him afterwards enabling him to outrun Ahab's chariot (18:44-46)? Jezebel's threat was all he could think about. Elijah went alone "a day's journey into the wilderness…and prayed that he might die" (4). God let him sleep and then sent an angel to bake fresh bread for him. It was comfort food; after filling his stomach and quenching his thirst, Elijah went back to sleep.

Then the angel touched Elijah awake again saying, "Get up and eat, for the journey is too much for you" (7). It was the same bread, but "Strengthened by that food, he traveled forty days and forty nights until he reached Horeb, the mountain of God" (8).

The root meaning of the word "companion" is to share bread. Elijah's bread-baking angel reminds me of Jesus sharing bread with two bewildered companions in Emmaus, knowing the journey was too much for them.

For over 40 years Jesus' followers have gathered at The Potter's House in Washington DC, companioning one another and welcoming strangers, serving delicious homemade meals with hot wheat rolls or cornbread. Some come in need of comfort and leave with amazing new strength for the journey to meet God.

Thank You God for Your comforting and invigorating sustenance. Thank You for fresh-baked bread and for companions with whom to share.

Soul Bread – 1

"Why spend money on what is not bread, and your labor on what does not satisfy? Listen, listen to me, and eat what is good, and your soul will delight in the richest of fare."

—Isaiah 55:2

GOD SPEAKS THROUGH the prophet Isaiah to his people like a wise parent concerned about a teenager blowing his whole paycheck on junk food. But he is talking about bread for the soul.

Imagine people today justifying themselves in response to God's question. One says, "I think I do spend my money, time and energy on **what is** bread, what will supply my needs; I *am* satisfied." He may not understand spiritual food, and his self-righteousness may blind him to his spiritual destitution. Another says, "I don't think there is any real, life-giving bread or possibility of satisfaction in life, at least for me." She may be overwhelmed by physical needs, and wealthy Christians may have turned her against Christianity. You and I could say: "Of course I'm satisfied; I'm successful and respected; I provide for my family, go to church and pay my tithe." Or: "This talk about being satisfied is pie-in-the-sky; most people on the planet are malnourished, sick and dying while the few rich want still more."

These viewpoints pollute our souls like high fructose corn syrup in mass-produced bread made for profit, not for nourishment. Are we buying into complacency, cynicism or despair? How desperately we need the soul health that only God's Word can stimulate!

God does not speak in harsh judgment, but with a gracious invitation to a daily feast. Because he became one of us in Jesus, he knows we waste resources, our priorities are askew and we often can't see beyond the tangible. As we delve into the Bible, its master author, God the Holy Spirit, guides us to see our motives, recognize our deep soul hunger, and come to him in repentance. Experiencing the unparalleled satisfaction of forgiveness and renewal, we delight in divine treasures of love and wisdom.

Holy Provider, may our needy souls feed on Your pure, life-nourishing Word today.

Soul Bread - 2

"It is written: 'People do not live on bread alone, but on every word that comes from the mouth of God.'"

—Matthew 4:4

JESUS, GOD'S WORD made flesh, a.k.a. the living bread, "was led by the Spirit into the wilderness to be tempted by the devil" (1). There Jesus was fortified by the words his loving Father had spoken at his baptism: "This is my Son, whom I love; with him I am well pleased" (Matthew 3:17). There the Holy Spirit, who had landed on his head in the form of a dove, nourished Jesus with the words of all the Hebrew Scriptures he had studied and discussed as a Jewish youth. For forty days and nights Jesus fasted from physical food and feasted on food he would tell his disciples, "you know nothing about" (John 4:32).

Therefore, when the devil tried to tempt him to take the easy way out and use his divine power to turn stones to bread, Jesus was ready with Scripture he had digested for himself as a human being. He quoted Moses, who told the Israelites: "God led you all the way in the wilderness these forty years, to humble and test you…, to teach you that people do not live on bread alone but on every word that comes from the mouth of the Lord" (Deuteronomy 8:2, 3).

What about us? What do we live on? Are our bodies overfed while our souls starve? Is the Spirit leading us to a wilderness experience to be humbled and tested? Do we need to fast from fast food and feast on God's Word? A balanced diet feeds whole persons, body and soul.

Bread of Life, thank You for stimulating my spiritual taste buds today.

Praying for Bread

"Give us today our daily bread."

—Matthew 6:11

HOW IS EVERYONE *this* morning?" Ann's enthusiastic question gets us off to a good start at the senior center. At 81, Ann lives by the day, rising at 4:30 AM to pray. We respond with "fine" or "OK" or "not sure yet" and ask how she is. Ann replies, "I'm blessed by the Best and glad to be here for another day."

The emphasis is on "today" or "daily" in this brief petition at the center of the prayer Jesus taught his disciples. Like Ann we all need to acknowledge, humbly and gratefully, that each day, with the energy to live it, is God's gift. Asking for *today*, rather than tomorrow or next week, helps us focus on *needs* rather than *wants*. Only God knows what we need and when.

The word "give" is not a demand or desperate plea. It is a humble yet confident request from beloved children to the Creator Sustainer of the universe, who is our loving Father because of Jesus' sacrifice. And we notice that Jesus teaches us to use "us" and "our," rather than "me" and "my." Next time we say (I mean *pray*) The Lord's Prayer, let us be in solidarity with hungry people as well as with Ann and all who know God's daily goodness.

Father in heaven, give us and those for whom we pray what You know we need today.

God's Bread

"I am the living bread that came down from heaven. Whoever eats of this bread will live forever."

—John 6:51

THREE DAYS BEFORE Aunt Ruthie died she stopped eating. The deathbed vigil with my father was similar. But they never stopped feeding on the bread of life. Ruthie's last words (with her eyes closed) were, "It's so beautiful!" Dad drew his last breath as Mom read to him from *Just Give Me Jesus*, by Anne Graham Lotz, a reflection on Jesus' words to Martha, "I am the resurrection and the life."

Beyond the idea that "seeing is believing" at a deeper level, believing is eating. Throughout our lives we come to know and trust the Savior more as the Holy Spirit energizes and synchronizes our hearts and minds to feed on Jesus. Nutrition experts say "you are what you eat." When we get sick, friends ask, "Was it something you ate?" The more we eat of the living bread, the more we become like Jesus, one with him in his life, death and resurrection. But when we consume the dead bread of merely human heroes or philosophies, our souls get sick.

Reading is like eating too. Eugene Peterson, author of *The Message Bible*, wrote a book called *Eat This Book* about chewing on God's Word and digesting it into the marrow of our lives.

Old Testament appetizers such as the manna in the wilderness offer foretastes of vital heavenly flavor. Jesus is the main course in Scripture's sumptuous banquet.

Living Bread, let more people throughout the world partake of You today.

Holy Bread

"Is not the bread that we break a participation in the body of Christ?

—1 Corinthians 10:16

OVERHEARING A SIX year old ask his mother, "When can I start taking the magic bread?" I pondered in our hushed circle around the table. The minister broke, lifted for God's blessing, and passed the bread, repeating solemnly, "the body of Christ, the bread of heaven." When his hand rested on the child's head in blessing, I prayed that the boy and his mother would realize love and joy overflowing. As we stood and chewed that bite silently and simultaneously, I prayed that throughout the days and weeks ahead we would share our lives, worship God, sing, pray and work together in the name of the one who gave up his life for us. I gave thanks that the child knew this bread was special. I prayed that all of us would distinguish between magic and miracle, between mysterious ritual and grateful, humble living.

At home I looked in the dictionary and found that the words *bread* and *break* were related. It reminded me that part of our participation in the body of Christ is accepting and sharing our brokenness, coming before God as sinners, all equally in need of Christ's atoning sacrifice.

Lord Jesus, thank You for Your love for children. May we come to You as children, eager and full of wonder.

Victory Bread

Read Revelation 2:12-17.

> "To those who are victorious, I will give some of the hidden manna…."
>
> —**Revelation 2:17**

FOR ATHLETES STRAINING to do their best in spite of overwhelming odds, whispered praises from teammates or coach can drown out the crowd's roar. In Pergamum, one of seven churches Jesus addressed through the apostle John, the crowd worshiped the emperor. Jesus, who had endured Roman torture and risen victorious, encouraged Christians to persevere in their counter-cultural faith in spite of the risk of martyrdom.

Most journeys of faith in Christ are not leisurely walks on the beach. We all need to hear Jesus' encouraging words. The aroma of his mystery bread lifts our spirits. By his Holy Spirit, Jesus, the bread of life, transforms our flagging hope to vigorous faith. His Word nourishes our souls with renewed capacity for joy, praise, wisdom and love, no matter how gloomy and scary the situation.

The word "manna" originally meant "what is it?" because the Israelites could not identify the food God rained down from heaven (Exodus 16:15, 31 and text note).

Our hearts see the mysteries of victory and eternal sustenance only dimly now. With childlike eagerness I anticipate looking into Jesus' eyes as he gently wipes my tears and gives me a piece of the hidden manna. No longer a mystery nourishment, I imagine a feast of creativity-generating, victory celebration bread.

Lord Jesus, thank You for Your sure promises. We long to see You face to face.

One in Christ

"…in Christ we, though many, form one body, and each member belongs to all the others."

—Romans 12:5

BEFORE *E PLURIBUS UNUM*—from many, one—our motto as Christians is "from one, many." Christ Jesus is the one, God's Messiah, anointed by the Holy Spirit. He is the only leader who generates life, growing his own diverse, worldwide body.

To be a Christian is to be "in Christ," dying daily to selfishness and being resurrected to live in love. Which is why my heart breaks and flies to the refugee mother dying of AIDS, whose picture I see in the paper, and also spills out in greetings to neighbors walking their dogs. Being in Christ is being in love with God. Living, moving and having our being in Christ, we are also in love with people. We care about each person on earth, can identify with them in some way, and feel compassion toward each one, especially the most needy. I sign my letters to incarcerated Crossroad Bible Institute students "Your Sister-in-Christ."

This being in love with God and all people is impossibly overwhelming on our own. Here's where "from many, one" comes in. We are baptized into Christ's Church. We are anointed with the Holy Spirit and given gifts, which energize us to work together, putting love in action.

In reflecting on words of familiar songs, I sometimes modify and personalize the word: For example, I know I'm a Christian by my love. I am astounded by love propelling me toward God and people in new ways each day.

Holy Head of the Church, keep reforming and uniting us to be Your faithful Body.

Christ Crucified

Read 1 Corinthians 1:18-31.

"Christ the power of God and the wisdom of God."
—1 Corinthians 1:24

OLD HYMNS LIKE "Jesus, Keep Me Near the Cross" and "When I Survey the Wondrous Cross" may sound anything but powerful or wise. Yet we "who are being saved" can sing them with fully engaged hearts and minds. One of my favorites is "In the Cross of Christ I Glory."

After years of repetition, the lyrics, like ubiquitous cross pendants or ornaments, may sentimentalize the Christ crucified whom Paul preached. New songs and poems can bring us back to the crux of the matter—that "God made foolish the wisdom of the world" and that "the weakness of God is stronger than human strength."

A four-line poem by John Thomas Carlisle expresses the paradox well:

They had to kill him
to stop him.
They did
and they didn't.

Christ Jesus, we praise You, all-powerful, all-wise, all-loving, ever-living!

Christ Alive in Me

"I have been crucified with Christ and I no longer live, but Christ lives in me."

—Galatians 2:20

PAUL'S RADICAL CLAIM is true for every Christian though we may not proclaim it like he did. As we become followers of Jesus, whether suddenly or over years of being "almost persuaded," we come into Christ, and by the Holy Spirit Christ permeates us. Not a warm fuzzy sensation, this is meltdown. We become "dead to sin, but alive to God in Christ Jesus" (Romans 6:11).

Sue Tinsley Robinson of Dexter, Missouri burned her "Erotic Temptations" porn shop inventory valued at $6,500. She continued as proprietor, but the store, renamed "Heaven's Grace: Bible, Bridal and Lace," was clearly under new (divine) management, as was Sue's life (*Today's Christian* January-February 2007).

Often the death-to-life transformation is less obvious. Psychologist Scott Peck called his Christian baptism a drowning, as he died to other religious traditions which had nourished him ("On Being a Christian" at www.mscottpeck.com). Those of us whose parents were devoted believers and who were baptized as infants still need to make a conscious decision to renounce the empty life outside of Christ's body and affirm the new spirited life within.

Live in me today, Lord; live in Your Church. Possess, infuse, inspire, us for enthusiastic life.

Filled with Christ

"... become mature, attaining to the whole measure of the fullness of Christ."

—Ephesians 4:13

HOW WAS CHURCH?" my son Christopher asked over supper
Monday. "It was good," I replied, then paused wondering what
details to offer. "Great sermon and a full house for communion."

The apostle Paul names four or five leadership gifts Christ gives
"to train Christians in skilled servant work...until we're all moving
rhythmically and easily with each other, efficient and graceful in
response to God's Son...fully developed within and without, fully
alive like Christ" (12, 13 MSG).

How do we know when a church is grown up? What makes a
church or worship service good? Four times in three verses Paul
points to Christ, and we realize that a church is mature to the degree that its members and actions are enlivened by Christ's Spirit.
There may not be a "full house" or a "full-orbed ministry," but
wherever people wholeheartedly and faithfully serve the one who
came to bring "life to the full" (John 10:10), Christ is forming a
mature community.

"But we missed you," I told Christopher. "And I missed being
there," he responded.

*Thank You Jesus for Your Church. Draw us into fuller ripeness
by Your anointing.*

Christ Defines Life

"For to me, to live is Christ and to die is gain."
—Philippians 1:21

I T'S A WIN/ win situation for Paul and for all of us who view life and death from a Spirit-informed perspective. Christ's new life surges in our spirits, releasing us from paralyzing fears of physical weakness and death. Neither do we long for death as an escape hatch, because every day brings new joys, new insights, renewed love of life, love of God and love of people.

In answer to the question, "What if Christ had not come?" Crossroad Bible Institute students often write, "I'd be dead," referring to suicide or homicide attempts, drug overdose or car crashes. People who have come close to dying usually appreciate life more intensely. In the same way we who every day "put to death" our decaying, dead-end, ego-engrossed ways of life rejoice in Christ's love-powered ever-growing vitality!

Today's English Version puts it this way: "For what is life? To me, it is Christ. Death, then, will bring more." We talk about people "passing away." That sounds too sad. Some just say, "she passed," which may be better since it reminds us of passing a test, graduating or proceeding to the next level of education. Yet heaven is not a kind of afterlife limbo of unending study. Paul and all in Christ know that to die is gain, for we will reign with Christ in unimaginable glory on the new earth.

Dear Master, we look forward to each new day with You, no matter what happens.

Always Christ

"Jesus Christ is the same yesterday and today and forever."
—Hebrews 13:8

THIS GRAND TESTIMONY links the writer's advice on godly leadership with a warning about "strange teachings." The tone is upbeat. Christ's eternal sameness is not what we would call the "same old, same old." Jesus is never boring and he never gets bored with us. Yet, unlike many human leaders, he does not act differently with different people. In fact, he does not "act." He is always authentic, loving, faithful, and his mercies are new every morning (Lamentations 3:23). He is always proactive, creating and recreating, reviving and renewing.

In the liturgy for Holy Communion, we profess: "Christ has died; Christ is risen; Christ will come again." The same one who created life, took on human life, gave up that life and was resurrected is the one who now offers everyone new permanent life. As we experience that life, we participate in and anticipate Christ's renewal of all things. In our own lives God's love in Christ redeems our past, enlivens our present and ensures our future.

For the Church, Christ's love is the origin or foundation, the structure, strength and vision. Throughout universal history, Christ the creator has been the life force, director and sustainer. The eternal future newness is mystery, but because of the timeless story of Jesus' love we know it will be good.

Lord Jesus Christ, may we and our leaders always follow You.

Christ Over All

"Grace and peace to you . . . from Jesus Christ, who is the faithful witness, the firstborn from the dead, and the ruler of the kings of the earth."

—Revelation 1:4-5

IT IS FEBRUARY, 2007. President Conte of Guinea in West Africa refuses to step down. This unjust ruler who grabbed his post in a military coup has rigged three elections to stay in power despite age and illness and is grooming his even more corrupt son to take over. Meanwhile the country devolves into the chaos of inflation, strikes, riots and looting. There is no grace and peace. What a contrast to Christ's kingdom!

The message given in John's vision reveals Christ Jesus as king over all earthly rulers. The apostle John transmits greetings as a humble emissary, giving all glory to the Christ, just as Roman messengers would give all honor to the Caesar.

As "the faithful witness" Jesus was supreme in speaking the truth of God's love and living it out to the point of being put to death. As "the firstborn from the dead" Jesus Christ will never die again, and all who look to him for life will live forever in his kingdom. Unlike earthly leaders, Jesus can be fully trusted to keep every promise, hide nothing, hoard nothing, tell all, give to all, empower all. And he will never need to step down. He is the fountain of infinite grace and peace.

Risen and reigning, glorious and gracious King, we praise You. Keep us faithful today.

Heart's Desires

"Take delight in the Lord, and he will give you the desires of your heart."

—Psalm 37:4

WHEN I WAS a single mom of three twenty-something kids, I thought that the desires of my heart were for all four of us to be happily married and then for me to have grandchildren living nearby. I was very familiar with this verse since my mom had given me a plaque engraved with it, which I had hanging in my bedroom; but I found it difficult to "delight myself in the Lord" until he started granting these desires.

Now ten years later I see that the truest desire of my heart was, and is, to take delight in God. Delighting in God, I enjoy life as the Holy Spirit keeps increasing my capacity to love and to be joyful in all circumstances.

If I had rushed into marriage before beginning to learn this delight, I believe that my desire to be married would have soon changed to the desire to be single. Instead, since my husband and I take daily delight in the Lord, we see our marriage as one of the best of our hearts' desires which God has given us.

Together we now have four adult children. We still have much to learn about delight and desires as we relate to our single sons, married daughter and son-in-law, and single mom daughter with our dear grandson. Delight in God multiplies our delight in other people and keeps us from judging them or expecting them to fulfill our desires.

Thank You Lord for showing me my desire to delight in You and enabling me to enjoy Your love with others.

Desires Fulfilled

Read Psalm 145.

> "He fulfils the desires of those who fear him; he hears their cry and saves them."
>
> **—Psalm 145:19**

EXPLORING HEBREW AND Greek concordances when studying Scripture helps quench my thirst to understand God's Word.

There are thirteen different Hebrew words for our noun "desire." In Psalm 145 David praises the King of all who provides for all. The same Hebrew word is used referring to God satisfying the desires of every living thing (16) and fulfilling the desires of those who fear him (19).

So is there a difference between satisfying and fulfilling? The Hebrew word used here for satisfy means *causing* to satisfy, and the one for fulfill means *to do*. There is a difference between ordinary desires and the thirst-for-righteousness desire of those who fear God. Maybe the translator understood that difference and thought that the English word "fulfill" better represented the way God himself satisfies our desires.

God created every creature with natural desires, wants or needs. God constantly ensures that these unspoken desires are satisfied, for animals and humans alike, for people who are unaware of him or ignore him as well as those who worship him in awe. But we who revere him realize that our deepest desire is to relate to God as our loving Father and Savior.

Lord God we thank You for satisfying and fulfilling every good desire. May we desire to know You better.

Pure Desire

"What a person desires is unfailing love; better to be poor than a liar."

—Proverbs 19:22

AT FIRST READING the two phrases in this proverb seem unrelated. My own struggle between true desire and deceptive wants can form the connection. God says: I understand your desires; all every person wants to have and to give is true love, kindness, generosity; I alone can provide and enable that love. Don't lie to yourself about riches or pretend to be wealthy when you're not.

The want ads used to be my favorite newspaper section. For years I searched those pages for the perfect job, for places to live, and even for a potential spouse. I was ashamed of my desires. How could I claim, "The Lord is my shepherd; I shall not want," and yet be addicted to want ads? I cried out to the Lord confessing my selfish ambition, coveting and lust, pleading for the Holy Spirit to purify my desires.

The false sheen of ads plays on empty desires for success, money or sex. Better that I realize my own poverty, my desperate need, my true heart's desire. God's Word and the loving people he brings into my life or into whose lives he leads me satisfy me like the want ads never could.

Lord, I love You and praise You for Your unfailing love. Keep me from being deceived, deceiving myself, entertaining illusions of grandeur.

Mature Desire

"Do not arouse or awaken love until it so desires."
—Song of Songs 8:4

A N AUNT'S OR grandmother's efforts to play matchmaker, hosting eligible men for dinner, may not be appreciated by a young woman. She may be wary of encouraging a man's advances, "leading him on" or "rushing things." A wise virgin waits for the maturation of her own desire as she develops true friendship with a man. She seeks God's will in prayer and meditation on Scripture, as well as the counsel of godly elders before considering a lifelong commitment in which body, mind and spirit are united.

Three times the woman in Song of Songs charges "the daughters of Jerusalem" not to "excite love, don't stir it up, until the time is ripe—and you're ready" (MSG). The Song of Songs is a beautiful, poetic dialog describing God's gift of love between a man and a woman. It can also portray God's love for each of us or Christ's for his bride, the Church.

Do I toy with God's affections? Have I entertained him for years, even enjoyed his attentions, but never desired what he desires, my total abandonment to him?

Lord Jesus, lover of my soul, take possession of me. May I desire and trust Your full-orbed love.

Desired Treasures

"I will shake all nations, and what is desired by all nations will come."

—Haggai 2:7

WHAT DO NATIONS desire? The hymn "Come, Thou Long-Expected Jesus" calls the Messiah "Israel's strength and consolation" and also "hope of all the earth...dear desire of every nation, joy of every longing heart" (Charles Wesley, 1744).

What is desired can be either a person or treasured things. Likewise glory and splendor can be attributed to a king or to a kingdom's material wealth. *The Amplified Bible* footnotes Haggai's prophecy explaining that since the verb "will come" is plural the "desired" designates treasures such as were brought by the wise men to Jesus.

Separation of church and state is necessary to prevent corruption, arrogance, greed and violence. No human ruler deserves to receive or can be trusted to administer the valued resources and treasures of all nations.

How we long for the new Jerusalem coming down from heaven, the time when Jesus, King of all kings, rules forever on the new earth! God will "shake down" all nations, causing all rulers to tremble before him and eagerly turn over their assets to the Prince of Peace. The prophet Isaiah foretells: "Then you will look and be radiant, your heart will throb and swell with joy; the wealth on the seas will be brought to you, to you the riches of the nations will come" (Isaiah 60:5).

We praise You, Judge and King of all the earth. We long for that time when the kingdoms and treasures of this world are turned over to You.

Last Desires

"I have eagerly desired to eat this Passover with you before I suffer."

—Luke 22:15

FOR TEN YEARS Ina battled cancer and kept up her teaching as well as family and church activities. When all treatments were exhausted she made one last trip with her husband to spend a weekend with their two-year-old grandson. Two months later she rejoiced to celebrate her husband's sixtieth birthday as family and friends gathered from out of state and overseas.

The approach of death can intensify and clarify desires. We want to be with people we love. We are eager to express our love for them and to know they love us. We want our life to have lasting significance. Above all we want to know that the people we love will be alive with us in heaven forever.

The "upper room discourses" culminating in the Lord's Supper have been called Jesus' last will and testament. Jesus the Godman sanctifies human friendship and the intimacy of table fellowship by expressing and fulfilling his desire to share his last meal with his disciples.

Ina's home-going memorial service was another joyous occasion for those of us who were assured that we will join her and all who have gone before to be with Jesus forever, where the feast "finds fulfillment in the kingdom of God" (16).

Thank You Father for satisfying our desires for close friendship and family, especially as we face death. Thank You, Jesus, for loving Your friends in spite of their forsaking You.

Spiritual Desires

Read 1 Corinthians 13 and 14.

> "Follow the way of love and eagerly desire spiritual gifts, especially the gift of prophecy."
>
> —1 Corinthians 14:1

HOW CAN SOMEONE tell us what to desire? Isn't desire spontaneous? Desires arise from our hearts which can be possessed by the Holy Spirit or tugged every which way by evil spirits like pride or envy. Parents can influence young children's desires by monitoring their own desires and talking about what is worth desiring. In the same way pastors, teachers and mentors can influence our desires.

The apostle Paul writes as a spiritual father to believers in Corinth who desired the gift of speaking in tongues. From his experience and as a prophet speaking God's Spirit-breathed Word of truth, Paul advocates love as the highest aspiration. He affirms the desire for spiritual gifts only if motivated by and exercised in love. Finally he shows how speaking in tongues is less loving both to fellow believers and less effective in witness to nonbelievers. Prophecy, the clear communication of God's truth, is the gift Paul urges them to desire. Yet "if I have the gift of prophecy and can fathom all mysteries and all knowledge, and if I have a faith that can move mountains, but do not have love, I am nothing" (13:2).

Last night on a public television news broadcast I saw a mother in Haiti making mud-pies of powdery soil she had scraped from a clay bank and mixed with a little butter and salt. When I saw her feed them to her children, a pang of compassionate and prophetic desire pierced my heart. I wanted to speak out and show the world how this mother's love and that of so many others is being violated.

Help me to examine my motives, Lord. Purify my desires. May I boldly speak the truth of Your unconditional love.

Down-to-earth Creativity

"In the beginning God created the heavens and the earth."
—Genesis 1:1

IT WAS MY first day of retirement. Now I would have plenty of time to write. Ideas and motivation from God's Word, other Christian writers, family and friends flooded my mind. I kept praying for guidance, but only managed several false starts, pages of scrawled brainstorms with more words and phrases crossed out than retained.

Finally I went out for a walk. Fortified by the sound of my footsteps on the dirt path, I smiled into the sunny sky and praised God, the source of my creativity. I thanked him for grounding me in his world, keeping me down-to-earth and delighting in his creation. I confessed that without the light of his Holy Spirit my writing was "formless and empty" like the earth before the first day (Genesis 1:2).

Whether we write, paint, sing or glorify God in other creative ways, he gives us two amazing sources of inspiring revelation: his created universe and his holy Word. Delving into Scripture increases our devotion to the Word made flesh, and learning about the cosmos increases our awe of this Word, who was there in the beginning and through whom all things were made (see John 1:1-3).

The "heavens" are incomprehensibly vast. In comparison the earth is miniscule. Yet God created the earth as a wonderful place for us to thrive. I don't need to know how or when the creation began, only who is the Creator and how I can respond to him in humility and gratitude.

Loving Creator, I love Your creation. Holy Spirit, I love Your Word. Thank You, Father, for creativity.

Down-to-earth Promise

"As long as the earth endures, seedtime and harvest, cold and heat, summer and winter, day and night will never cease."
—Genesis 8:22

MAI WORKS A twelve-hour shift in a chilly, windowless factory, stitching seams, inserting the "Made in China" labels. Throughout the winter, Sundays are her only times to see daylight. Often she recalls the years before her parents died when they used to watch sunrises and sunsets together.

Each Sunday Mai hurries to the secret place where her church family meets. This week the message is from Genesis, God's promise to Noah after the flood. After enjoying a feast of rice and vegetables harvested last fall from members' gardens, Mai walks the eight kilometers back to her flat.

The sun sets in hues far more glorious than any of the colorful fabrics at the factory. Mai rejoices in the beauty and goodness of God's creation. She gives thanks for God's faithfulness as she looks forward to the light and warmth of spring when the beans will sprout in her window box.

On the bus ride to work Monday, Mai praises God as she delights in the light of the morning star above the setting moon. She will have lots to talk about with the women who sit near her at the sewing machines.

(Note: Although this story is pure fiction, I trust the Holy Spirit formed it in my imagination.)

Father in heaven, thank You for the reliability and rhythms of nature which affirm Your love to us each day.

Down-to-earth Prayer – 1

Read Job 38 – 41.

> **"Do you know the laws of the heavens? Can you set up God's dominion over the earth?"**
>
> —Job 38:33

LIKE JOB WE want answers. When we suffer we want somebody to blame. Our prayers keep demanding "Why?" and "Enough already!"

Job's three friends "sat on the ground with him" for a week in silence (Job 2:13). But after Job vents his frustration, each of them lecture and argue about how you can't blame God; he must be punishing you. Job insists he doesn't deserve it and prays for an audience with God. Finally after a fourth (younger, but slightly wiser) friend speaks up, God speaks to Job at length "out of the storm."

Amazing! God, the creator of the universe, speaks in understandable words to a human being on earth! But God does not answer Job's question. God does not tell him how he had spoken highly to Satan of "my servant Job" and then agreed to let Satan test Job's faith by destroying his family, wealth and health. Instead God asks Job who he thinks he is and about fifty more rhetorical questions, contrasting human logic and perspective with the genius and vastness of God's rule as revealed in creation and its creatures.

Maybe we need to pray outdoors more often, as people like Abram, Moses, David and Job did. It's a good way to humble ourselves, allow God to put us in our place and take us down to size, away from manmade technology we rely on and revere. When others suffer, maybe we could sit in silence with them for awhile outdoors.

Holy Creator, turn our minds from our own suffering to Your majesty and love.

Down-to-earth Prayer – 2

Read Habakkuk 2.

> "For the earth will be filled with the knowledge of the glory of the Lord as the waters cover the sea."
>
> —Habakkuk 2:14

EVERY MORNING JOE'S grandmother kneels in her assisted living apartment pleading for Joe. She prays for her children and other grandchildren as well; she prays for missionaries she knows and the people with whom they minister; she prays for seekers, backsliders and new Christians among her acquaintances—all by name. Today this persistent widow eagerly claims God's promise that the whole earth will brim over with "awareness of God's glory" (MSG).

Joe is an environmentalist. He hasn't been in church since he left for college twelve years ago. But today Joe agrees to visit his girlfriend's church since she's been raving about their sermons and work projects. The round sanctuary with its many windows and skylights open to trees and clouds impresses Joe. He appreciates seeing so many people of all ages and races together. The music is irresistible as everyone sings like kids at a pep rally a song about trees clapping. It is the words of Scripture that magnetize him: "The Lord is in his holy temple; let all the earth be silent before him" (20).

Joe recalls his sense of awe in the predawn hush as he walks to the bird sanctuary each morning and the indescribably wild joy he feels watching tree branches move in breezes. From now on he will freely express that awe and joy in praise and worship of the Creator. That afternoon he will call his grandmother and thank her for her prayers.

Thank You Lord God that all nature sings Your praise. Open our ears and the ears of our children's hearts to hear and join in the music of the spheres.

Down-to-earth Landowners

"Blessed are the meek, for they will inherit the earth."
—Matthew 5:5

AFTER SLAVERY WAS abolished in the United States, some
former slaves who had close ties with their former masters
eventually became landowners. But the "forty acres and a mule"
grants were rescinded as President Andrew Johnson pardoned ex-
confederates and returned their land to them. In contrast, both
David in Psalm 37 and Jesus in the Sermon on the Mount describe
a last-shall-be-first happy ending in God's kingdom.

Who are the meek today? Who will inherit the renewed earth?
The meek are those whose lives are not motivated primarily by
greed, being "content with just who you are" (MSG); "patient, long-
suffering" (AB); "those who claim nothing" (Phillips) knowing they
are totally dependent on God; "those of a gentle spirit" (NEB).

David's promise, "Those who are evil will be destroyed, but
those who hope in the Lord will inherit the land" (Psalm 37:9),
is confirmed by the apostle John: "The time has come for judging
the dead, and for rewarding...your people who revere your name,
both great and small—and for destroying those who destroy the
earth" (Revelation 11:18).

I believe that in this time of the earth's awful pollution and
exploitation, the meek are people who acknowledge "The earth
is the Lord's, and everything in it" (Psalm 24:1). In humility they
respect and value God's creation. No wonder Jesus promises to
bequeath it to them; he knows they will care for it.

*Forgive our thoughtless arrogance, Lord. Teach us the joys of
meekness and earth-keeping.*

Down-to-earth Kingdom

"…your kingdom come, your will be done on earth as it is in heaven."

—Matthew 6:10

MY FATHER OR mother prayed aloud with us at the table before each meal. But on Sunday evening they would lead us in praying "The Lord's Prayer" in unison. We also prayed this prayer in church sometimes, probably when we had communion and maybe in Sunday school.

That was fifty years ago. Since then I have heard sermon series, read books on The Lord's Prayer and prayed it thousands of times alone and in groups of various sizes. Finally I am beginning to consider how I mean what I pray.

The Benedictine motto, *Ora et Labora*—Pray and Work, helps me pray this prayer sincerely. I long for God's rule and purposes to be carried out on earth, where humankind has stewardship, even as in the vast unseen realm where God is totally and directly in charge. Being sincere about this kingdom-come petition means yielding to God rather than to the forces of materialism, convenience, and efficiency. It means *working* to conserve and restore the earth. How thankful I am for Christian organizations like A Rocha International and the Evangelical Environmental Network!

Lord, we long for the time when all the kingdoms of this world will become Your kingdom. Strengthen us to be good stewards of the earth.

Down-to-earth Vision

**"Then I saw a new heaven and a new earth; for the first heaven
and the first earth had passed away...."**

—Revelation 21:1

OFTEN THROUGHOUT THE Bible heaven or the heavens and
earth are coupled in a sentence or phrase. The apostle John's
like the prophet Isaiah's description of the new heaven and earth
points to the ultimate physical and spiritual unity of these now
disparate spheres (Isaiah 65:17). The last verse of a favorite hymn
yearns for that eternal reality:

> *This is my Father's world:*
> *The battle is not done;*
> *Jesus who died shall be satisfied,*
> *And earth and heaven be one.*
> *—Maltbie D. Babcock, 1901*

John's visions and other biblical references to end times generate
more questions than answers. What of the first earth which God
created and called "very good?" Could it be one and the same as
the new one, paradise resurrected? The Bible's apocalyptic prophecies do not excuse our trashing the planet any more than our own
approaching demise gives us license to take suicidal risks, pollute
our body, or ignore our health. Rather than being destroyed with
"those who destroy the earth" (Revelation 11:18), the vision of
the new unified heaven and earth inspires us to join Jesus who is
already "making all things new" (Revelation 21:5).

*Lord God, thank You for creating us and the earth, our home.
We praise You for recreating us and revealing Your vision for
the new creation.*

Free to Live and Learn

"I run in the path of your commands, for you have set my heart free."

—Psalm 119:32

BRITISH STATESMAN THOMAS Macaulay dubbed the principle "no people ought to be free till they are fit to use their freedom" as foolish as someone refusing to go into the water until he learns to swim (*The New Dictionary of Thoughts*, 1957).

Knowing that we can only learn by doing, God created human beings with free will. Why then did the psalmist need his heart set free? And what is free about keeping to a prescribed path or obeying certain commandments? The problem with free will is we choose unwisely much of the time, unaware that our hearts are captivated by demons. Heart freedom is a double gift: God frees us *from* ego trips, guilt trips, mistakes, regrets, grudges, restlessness and fear; God frees us *to* love, forgiveness, wisdom, gratitude and joy. Instead of trudging blindly and doggedly away from God and people, we begin to "run in the path" of free-hearted love of God and people.

With Jesus we wade into the living water of God's commands. Before we realize it, by the power of God the Holy Spirit, we are swimming in deep refreshing pools.

Lord Jesus, thank You for a free heart to know and love and follow You.

Free to Heal and Give Life

"Heal the sick, raise the dead, cleanse those who have leprosy, drive out demons. Freely you have received, freely give."
—Matthew 10:8

JESUS FREED HIS disciples to interact with people in a new way. He commissioned them to serve him in freeing others. The foundation of this freeing life was the divine authority of Jesus' teaching. Jesus' public demonstration of his astounding imperatives freed his disciples from doubt, motivating and empowering them for confident, compassionate, generous ministry.

I wonder how soon or how many of the twelve tapped into Jesus' power to free people from disease, demon possession and death itself. Luke writes about the situation soon after Jesus' ascension and the outpouring of the Holy Spirit: "Everyone was filled with awe at the many wonders and signs performed by the apostles" (Acts 2:43). And stories of saints throughout history, beginning with the apostle Paul, reveal God's suspension of the "laws of nature," freeing his followers to be instrumental in freeing others from all kinds of ailments.

Does Jesus still commission apostles and miracle-workers today? Does my preoccupation with when or how this new life of freedom is expressed keep me from freely receiving and freely giving? Am I deaf to Jesus' call to minister to people suffering with deadly addictions or mental illness today?

Thank You Jesus for Your gifts. May I receive and share them freely.

Free to Love

"The Spirit of the Lord is on me because he has anointed me
…to proclaim freedom for the prisoners and recovery of sight
for the blind, to set the oppressed free…."

—Luke 4:18

IMAGINE JESUS READING his own commission in these words
from the book of Isaiah. His voice communicates joy and love. He
envisions pastors in many countries imprisoned and tortured yet
truly free, singing like Paul and Silas in Philippi. He sees criminals
serving life sentences reading this same good news and knowing
they are eternally free in spirit.

Imagine Jesus seeing *himself* bound before Pilate, mocked,
scourged and nailed on a cross, freely choosing to love and forgive
no matter the cost. "For the joy set before him he endured the
cross…" (Hebrews 12:2).

Jesus knows he will live out that liberating joy in resurrection
from death, ascension to heaven and ruling the universe forever.
But because Jesus embodies love, his penultimate joy is in seeing
penitent sinners forgiven, freed to give and receive love—"there is
rejoicing in the presence of the angels of God over one sinner who
repents" (Luke 15:7). Imagine Jesus seeing the thief on the cross
as he proclaims himself to be Isaiah's promised liberator.

*Lord, have You also anointed us to proclaim Your freedom
from blindness, captivity and oppression? Free us to hear, see
and respond.*

Free to Know and Be Known

"If you hold to my teaching, you are really my disciples. Then you will know the truth, and the truth will set you free."
—John 8:31-32

IN THE MOVIE *I Am Sam*, the boy escapes from a work camp in Bulgaria. But until he knows the truth about who he is, he is not free. That truth, his documented identity, is sealed in an envelope, a gift from the man who helped him escape.

In a sense we are like Sam. On our own initiative and with help from kind people we may manage to escape tyrannies such as poverty, injustice, even ignorance. But until we know who we are, we are not free. We need to know where we came from and where we are going. Otherwise we are lost and in bondage to fear.

Sam needed to know who his parents were and that they loved him. He needed his birth certificate or passport to travel freely from one country to another. Our truest identity is as children of God and disciples of Jesus. As Sam held on to his papers, we need to "hold on to" Jesus' teachings. The Bible certifies our spiritual birth, emancipation and adoption into God's worldwide family—everything we need to move freely across all life's borders.

The more we explore our rich heritage in Scripture, the more free we become in expressing joy and love. Like Sam when he began to realize people cared about him, we will learn how to smile again; we will begin to trust and care for people rather than fear, envy or despise them.

Set us free, Lord Jesus, and we will be truly free. Thank You for showing us all we need to know in Your Word.

Free to be Renewed

"Now the Lord is the Spirit, and where the Spirit of the Lord is, there is freedom."

—2 Corinthians 3:17

MINNIE IS A free spirit. At 85 she lives alone, has no family, and can no longer drive. But she refuses to be labeled "homebound" or a "shut-in." Every day friends are blessed by her smile, her humor and her love, whether in person or by phone.

Lillian is an even more surprising free spirit. Confined to a wheelchair or bedridden for over three years, she cannot even feed herself now, due to Lou Gehrig's disease. Yet she never complains and always expresses loving concern about the health of her visitors and their friends or family.

What is Minnie's and Lillian's secret? "Where the Spirit of the Lord is, there is freedom." These women are losing control of their physical lives. But their self-control flourishes, along with love, joy, peace, patience and the other fruits of the Spirit.

The word free can also mean willing or generous. King David prayed: "Restore to me the joy of your salvation and grant me a willing spirit, to sustain me" (Psalm 51:12)—"uphold me by Your generous Spirit" (NKJV). Minnie and Lillian are willing, generous, free spirits, upheld and sustained by the Spirit of the Lord. They know, have personally experienced, that Jesus Christ, the son of God, has set them free, and they are "free indeed" (John 8:36).

Thank You Lord for the testimony of those who may be restricted or even paralyzed in body but shine with Your free Spirit.

Free to Welcome Others

"It is for freedom that Christ has set us free. Stand firm then, and do not let yourselves be burdened again by a yoke of slavery."

—Galatians 5:1

PAUL'S EPISTLE ON freedom in Christ warns Gentile Christians to steer clear of Judaizers, proponents of Jewish laws and ceremonies as requirements for believers.

Down through history there have always been people who set themselves up as gatekeepers and judges. They glorify tradition and set up litmus tests which preserve their own authority. Could we call them Christianizers? Martin Luther proclaimed freedom from the yoke of indulgences, celibacy for priests, and other Roman Catholic traditions. Women like Phoebe Palmer, Hannah Whitall Smith and Aimee Semple McPherson taught and preached, free of gender constrictions. At Azuza Street with black evangelist William Seymour, huge multiracial crowds worshiped, free of color and cultural barriers.

What walls do we erect today that elevate ourselves and make others second-class Christians? What social conventions do we use to measure new church members' morality? Are we, like the Judaizers, promoting salvation by human merit and discrimination rather than by God's grace? Paul's defense of freedom in Christ speaks to long-time Christians relating to ex-offenders, refugees, and other marginalized people who visit our churches.

Lord, keep us standing firm in solidarity with all those whose shackles You have removed.

Responsible Freedom

"Live as free people, but do not use your freedom as a cover-up for evil; live as God's slaves."

—1 Peter 2:16

"IT'S A FREE country, ain't it?" I can still hear the brash and bitter tone of this teenage exclamation uttered to justify lewd behavior and "free speech" laced with profanity.

God's kingdom is a free country which Jesus started and which is spreading throughout the world. Christ has freed those who belong to his kingdom from guilt and from the fear of judgment.

But freedom isn't free. It's always tied to responsibility. Peter warns believers not to use their freedom to excuse or rationalize rebellion against legal, God-ordained authorities. Paul also warned those "called to be free. . . do not use your freedom to indulge the sinful nature; rather serve one another humbly in love" (Galatians 5:13). Whenever we try to speak or act on our own authority we violate our human constitution and end up miserable. We were created to be subservient to God and to co-operate with people. These responsible relationships enable us to live in joyful freedom.

Only God is totally free. But in Jesus "he made himself nothing by taking the very nature of a servant" (Philippians 2:7).

Forgive our misuse of the spiritual freedom You won for us, Lord Jesus. Keep teaching us to serve You and each other freely in love.

Growing Flowers

"And why do you worry about clothes? See how the flowers of the field grow."

—Matthew 6:28

BEFORE EASTER EACH year a widow and her daughter arrange flowers and plants in our church narthex with a hand-lettered placard listing the names of deceased members. These women are not known for Easter hats and suits or stunning "Sunday clothes." They aren't known for anything; even their annual floral memorial is an anonymous tribute. They thrive on seeing—considering, enjoying, celebrating—rather than being seen.

Jesus teaches us to look at and learn from "the flowers of the field." Flowers, especially wildflowers, beam with growth. A grandparent seeing her grandchild after many months exclaims, "He's growing like a weed!"

Dandelions, daffodils and daisies teach us dependency on God, humility, vitality and beauty. Like the widow and her daughter, flowers thrive on seeing—absorbing sun, rain and soil nutrients—rather than being seen.

Worry and workaholism stunt growth. Fashions and fads only grow worries. Enjoy the flowers with Jesus!

Forgive my petty and self-centered concerns, Lord God. Thank You, Jesus, for flowers and people who care for them.

Growing Children

Read Luke 2:40-52.

> **"And as Jesus grew up, he increased in wisdom and in favor with God and people."**
>
> —Luke 2:52

LUKE WAS A holistic physician and the only Gospel writer who mentioned Jesus' boyhood. Before relating the story of Jesus interacting with temple scholars at age twelve, Luke summarizes Jesus' childhood as a time of mental and spiritual as well as physical growth (40). He rephrases the diagnosis at the end of the temple story, adding social growth (52).

Luke may have been alluding to another famous Hebrew boy who grew "in stature and in favor with the Lord and with people" (1 Samuel 2:26). According to Dr. Luke, young John the Baptist also became "strong in spirit" (Luke 1:80).

Do we as "grown-ups" tend to skim over these verses? If we are spiritually grown up, we will work to insure that no child's growth is cut off or stunted. We will encourage rather than condemn precocious children or restless youths.

Reflecting on the differences between age and maturity, wisdom and knowledge, grace and popularity can help us keep growing throughout our lives, rather than languishing in spiritual adolescence.

Holy Spirit, thank You for growth spurts and steady maturation in Your wisdom and grace.

God the Grower

Read 1 Corinthians 3:1 – 9.

> "I planted the seed, Apollos watered it, but God has been making it grow. So neither the one who plants nor the one who waters is anything, but only God, who makes things grow."
>
> —1 Corinthians 3:6-7

MULLING OVER THE words for these devotionals each day, I pray for growth:

Loving God, You know how I wake up feeling like a newborn baby, craving Your pure spiritual milk, so that by it I can grow up in salvation, now that I have tasted that You are good. (1 Peter 2:2,3).

Holy God who alone makes things grow, thank You for Jesus, Your living, breathing Word, who grew up before You like a tender shoot, and like a root out of dry ground (Isaiah 53:2). Thank You for Your Holy Spirit, who enabled the seeds of Your Word, planted by Paul, John, and many others, to take root in my heart. Thank You for Your faithful planters and waterers, through whose teachings and writings Your Word grows in me. Thank You for the desire and calling to plant or water Your seeds in others through my writing.

I confess my envy of better writers. I confess my failure to wait on You, to listen to You in my rush to finish and publish. Thank You for good editors and willing readers. May those who notice any growth in my writing ability give You all the praise.

Growing Church Members

Read Ephesians 4:7 -16.

> "…we will in all things grow up into him who is the head, that is, Christ."
>
> —**Ephesians 4:15**

PAUL REPEATS MAXIMIZING words—each, all, whole, fullness and every—in his efforts to envision church growth. But language fails him, for our head, the one who continuously and completely equips us, "ascended higher than all the heavens, in order to fill the whole universe" (10).

Church growth is not competitive like financial growth. Nor is personal growth in Christ limited like physical development. Churches grow as people identify more and more closely with Christ, humbly serving each other, pouring out our lives in love for each other as Jesus did. It's growth from inside-out and from outside-in, from top-down and from bottom-up, growth in all ways for each member, which in turn attracts new members. It's a steady, everyday growth as well as in growing seasons and growth spurts.

Today, and perhaps each week after being in church, it is good to ask myself a few questions: Am I growing up? Do I speak the truth in love? Am I involved in a "supporting ligament" ministry and a healthy congregation that "grows and builds itself up in love, as each part does its work" (16)?

Thanks for your equipment, Lord Jesus. Unite and grow us in your true love.

Growing Good News

"...the gospel is bearing fruit and growing throughout the whole world...."

—Colossians 1:6

MYSTERY RELIGIONS, SUPERSTITIONS and cults were popular in Paul's day. In contrast to their "hollow and deceptive philosophy" (Colossians 2:8) Paul proclaims the gospel (good news) truth of Jesus. It is a dynamic, fruit-bearing news because the seed is the living Word of God planted in individual hearts by the Holy Spirit of God. The message of Jesus' life, death, resurrection, and the coming of the Holy Spirit is the best possible news there ever was. It is the greatest, most irresistible love story relived in the lives of people of all races, ages and classes. In the thirty plus years after Jesus inaugurated it, the Christian Church grew rapidly throughout the then-known world of the Roman Empire.

Today the gospel has literally spread throughout the world. One-third of the earth's inhabitants are counted as Christians. Especially in Africa, Asia and South America "the gospel is bearing fruit and growing" both spiritually and in numbers of converts. Also the gospel's life-generating power is reviving and renewing churches in Europe and North America.

Lord Jesus, may your Word of truth bear fruit in my life today. Let the gospel's growth throughout the world encourage us in solidarity and witness.

Growing Faithful Love

"…your faith is growing more and more, and the love all of you have for one another is increasing."

—2 Thessalonians 1:3

THE PEOPLE OF Church A saw each other once a week at most and communicated even less. Attendance at Sunday school, worship services and Bible studies was dwindling. Occasionally a visitor from the church neighborhood showed up but then didn't return. Discouraged leaders kept up the routines; prayers stagnated.

Most people in the Church B family were in contact with someone from church twice or three times weekly. Couples prayed together daily. The seniors' Bible study, youth group, choir and various support or mission groups flourished as new people joined. It was a faithful friendship-building church and a visiting church. There were home visits, phone visits, hospital visits, school visits, prison visits and workplace visits. There were celebrations, walks, talks over breakfast, lunch or dinner and all kinds of recreational activities. Prayer and praise flowed freely wherever people gathered.

Surprisingly, Church A and Church B are one and the same, or rather Church B was once Church A. Similarly the Thessalonian church is known for growth in faith and love, whereas Paul was concerned about these qualities in their congregation earlier (1 Thessalonians 3: 5, 10, 12). It was prayer that made the difference. Faithful, continual, constant prayers of thanksgiving, confession and intercession reconnect churches to Christ our living head, producing growth in faith and love.

Lord Jesus Christ, thank You for hearing our prayers and reviving churches. Increase our faith and love.

Graceful Growth

"But grow in the grace and knowledge of our Lord and Savior Jesus Christ."

—2 Peter 3:18

IN CORRESPONDENCE WITH Crossroad Bible Institute students I often quote this verse as a prayer—"that you may grow...." Paul uses the imperative with apostolic authority. He urges growth in grace and knowledge of Jesus' truth as opposed to false teachings which were cropping up in church groups.

The Holy Spirit speaks to each of us today with this growth counsel. The tone does not convey a judgmental or condescending "Grow up. Act your age" admonition. Rather we hear a gentle, joyful encouragement to receive more of God's good gifts, more of the "grace and truth [that] came through Jesus Christ" (John 1:17).

We are invited to experience God's gracious forgiveness, loving welcome and unending generosity each day in new ways. It is an offer of lifelong learning to know God.

Signs of this growth in our lives will be wise, gracious words, hospitality, humility, discernment and love. This is my prayer for each of us. Whether we are senior citizen instructors or youthful inmates enrolled in a correspondence course of Bible study, whether we know a little or a lot, whether we are graceful and gracious or seemingly without grace, there is plenty of room for growth in knowing Jesus and living in his grace-filled love.

Use me today, Holy Spirit, to graciously encourage someone in knowing and loving Jesus.

Hope Plugged In

Read Psalm 42.

> "Why, my soul, are you downcast? Why so disturbed within me? Put your hope in God, for I will yet praise him, my Savior and my God."
>
> —Psalm 42:11

HOW DO WE get our hopes up when we feel discouraged? The psalmist talks to himself, telling his soul to put what little hope he has in God. In other versions he resolves to "wait for God" (NEB); he prays, "Fix my eyes on God" (MSG).

Hope is like a light bulb. It does no good without a lamp and electricity. To be hopeful we must have something to hope for and someone to hope in.

Some days I feel hopeless. I realize that in myself, no matter how much I study the Bible, go to church or pray, I am not optimistic; the future does not seem promising; my outlook is dim, my vision clouded; I am severely lacking in trust, confidence and faith. Then I realize that I've been carrying the hope light bulb of my soul around rather than connecting to the Holy Spirit of God.

God is not like electricity that goes out when there is a storm. What a relief to come to God and say, "You are my only hope; I'm hopeless without You!" As I sincerely confess my desire to put my hope in my creator, redeemer and soul lover, I start focusing on God's amazing revelations in creation and Scripture. Prayer, worship and Bible study radiate again with joyful beams of hope. Rather than feeling sorry for myself, I'm praising God, the infinite, eternal one.

Thank You Lord for turning my flimsy hope into strong faith. Keep me connected.

Hope Crying Out

"I rise before dawn and cry for help; I have put my hope in
your word."

—Psalm 119:147

KAREN WAKES AT 5 AM hearing her daughter Amy crying in
the next room. "Lord Jesus, you said 'Let the children come to
me.' Come with me to this one now," she prays. Twenty minutes
later Amy is sound asleep, bad dream banished by Karen's singing, "Jesus loves the little children..." (Clare Herbert Woolston
1856-1927).

As usual, Katherine in the house next door is awake at 5:30,
praying her way through the Psalms. Today this section of Psalm
119: "God! Answer! I'll do whatever you say. [I'm] crying for help,
hoping for a word from you" (145, 147 MSG).

Jesus himself could well have repeated this and many other
Psalm texts as he cried to his Abba for help "in childlike prayer"
(AB).

Whether we are parents, grandparents, early risers or insomni-
acs, hopeful believers or hopers against hope, our cries for help can
be expressions of hope rather than despair. As soon as we cry out
to God, appealing to his loving promises, trusting in his Word, the
Holy Spirit who inspired Scripture infuses our minds. God gives us
what we need to begin each day—a verse of Scripture, a song, an
idea, renewed energy, confidence to pray, or more sleep.

*"My soul faints with longing for your salvation, but I have put
my hope in your word," Lord God* (Psalm 119:81).

Hope Growing

"...suffering produces perseverance; perseverance, character; and character, hope. And hope does not put us to shame, because God's love has been poured out into our hearts...."

—Romans 5:3-5

PEOPLE WHO DON'T know Jim might call him a glutton for punishment. He spends twelve hours at work some days and has put in fifty-five-hour weeks plus being on call at home. Is Jim suffering? Not much, compared to the early Christians. But he is persevering at age sixty-three with no plans to retire. His enduring efforts to overcome all technical and interpersonal obstacles continue to shape the integrity of his character. Jim is hopeful, cheerful, upbeat because he daily experiences God's love. He trusts God more and more, supported by his wife's love, Christian coworkers, words of Scripture, many prayers and above all the Spirit's power.

The root meaning of character is to scratch, engrave or mark to indicate ownership, which reminds me of branding sheep and the horrible practice of branding slaves. Today character is defined as a "distinguishing attribute," a "complex of mental and ethical traits marking a person or group," and "moral excellence or firmness."

Either way suffering is involved. But whether the suffering produces perseverance, whether the perseverance produces character, and the character produces hope depends on whether the sufferers' hearts are revived continuously by God's love.

Let us be channels of Your love today, Lord God. Lead those who suffer along the way of hope.

Beaming Hope

"May the God of hope fill you with all joy and peace as you trust in him, so that you may overflow with hope by the power of the Holy Spirit."

—**Romans 15:13**

DUST OFF YOUR hope" read the subject line on an email from *Faithful Security: National Religious Partnership on the Nuclear Weapons Danger*. Christians have been hoping, praying and advocating for a nuclear-free world for years. Often our hopes do get "dusty" as nuclear stockpiles rise and disarmament initiatives fail. We need to intercede for one another, joining Paul in reliance on God for ever-bright hope, joy and peace.

"May God, the source of hope" (TEV) inspire our intercession. May the Holy Spirit "remove all bounds to hope" (JB) for us and those for whom we pray. May our "whole life and outlook be radiant with hope" (Phillips). Thank God, hope is contagious!

The Greek word for hope used here means confident expectation or anticipation with pleasure. We can always look forward to wonderful surprises. The God of hope says: "I have… plans to prosper you and not to harm you, plans to give you hope and a future" (Jeremiah 29:11).

Keep our hope fountains bubbling over, Lord. Energize us and our prayers, Holy Spirit.

Sober Hope

"But since we belong to the day, let us be sober, putting on faith and love as a breastplate, and the hope of salvation as a helmet."

—1 Thessalonians 5:8

WE ARE PEOPLE of the light. Paul calls us to face the future with both realism and optimism. Faith, hope and love form a solid armor that repels doubt, despair and evil. Helmets save lives. Where there is life there is hope.

We can't see our helmets when they are in place. Similarly, "hope that is seen is no hope" (Romans 8:24). But we can certainly experience the security of knowing Jesus has us covered. The Holy Spirit saves our minds from insanity, our brains from crashing with migraines due to overload or anxiety.

Our past and present deliverances from remorse, guilt and fear fuel our hope for the ultimate cosmic salvation. Our hope helmets come equipped with visionary goggles. Through their lens our perspective is purposeful; we live "in hope that the creation itself will be liberated from its bondage to decay and brought into the freedom and glory of the children of God" (Romans 8:20, 21).

Lord Jesus, we await Your return with sober yet high hopes.

Holding on to the Hope

Read Hebrews 10:19 – 25

> "Let us hold unswervingly to the hope we profess, for he who promised is faithful."
> —Hebrews 10:23

LIKE FAITH, HOPE is one of those old-time names. I don't know anyone named Hope though I've seen the name referring to women in the past or today among Christians outside of the United States.

Hebrews is a book of hope, proclaiming Jesus as the "better hope" (7:19), better than trying to obey divine laws or human regulations, the only viable, permanent link between God and humankind. The writer urges believers to persevere and "make your hope sure" (6:11 and 18; see also 3:6), calling our hope in Christ "an anchor for the soul, firm and secure" (6:19).

The Future of Hope: Christian Tradition amid Modernity and Postmodernity is a book of "hope retrieval" for our times. In their introduction, editors Miroslav Volf and William Katerberg challenge Christians "to rejuvenate a living hope rooted in the 'hot memory' of God's engagement with the world in Christ's life, death, and resurrection."

Our verse for today is the second of three "Let us" rallying calls: "let us draw near to God..." (22); "let's keep a firm grip on the promise" (verse 23—MSG); "let us consider how we may spur one another on..." (24, 25). I would add: Let's name a daughter Hope or a retirement home Hope House (as author Jan Karon did in her Mitford series); let's revive those beloved hymns, "Whispering Hope" and "My Hope Is Built" and write new songs of hope.

Thank You, Jesus, that in You "our anchor holds and grips the solid rock."

Hope with Answers

"Always be prepared to give an answer to everyone who asks you to give the reason for the hope that you have"
—1 Peter 3:15b

PEOPLE WHO USE the word hope a lot may not have living hope. Some use hope in an effort to influence others as in "I hope you will ...." Others respond to questions with, "I hope so," or modify expectations with "hopefully."

We who have been born again "into a living hope through the resurrection of Jesus Christ from the dead" (1 Peter 1:3) don't need to talk ourselves or others into a hopeful frame of mind. We will not only sound hopeful, people who know us will see that we live in hope every day. Our hope grows as we age through years of daily Spirit infusions and the prospect of our own resurrection day.

Peter is writing in a time of persecution, assuming Christians will need to "account for" and even "make a defense" for their faith (RSV); yet he uses the word hope. From personal experience Peter knew that Christians are known not only by their love but by the powerful hope they generate. He and John had been imprisoned and interrogated for healing a crippled beggar, resulting in Peter's courageous testimony before the Jewish leaders: "It is by the name of Jesus Christ of Nazareth, whom you crucified but whom God raised from the dead, that this man stands before you healed" (Acts 4:10).

Preparation for testifying about our hope is accomplished in the same way as reviving our hope—by conscious, wholehearted and continual reverence of "Christ as Lord" (15a). A person who makes self or someone else lord has a false or dead hope. No wonder hardly anyone is asking them to give the reason for it!

Jesus Christ, we praise you for the sure hope of resurrection life which energizes us as we worship You. May our hope be evident to all. Prepare us to answer.

Success and Integrity

"...walk before me faithfully with integrity of heart...."
—1 Kings 9:4

SOLOMON HAD EVERYTHING going for him. He was chosen by God not only to rule the kingdom of Israel which his father David had battled to establish, but also to build God's holy temple in Jerusalem. God even told Solomon in a dream: "Ask for whatever you want me to give you." Solomon humbly and wisely asked for wisdom—"a discerning heart to govern your people and to distinguish between right and wrong" (1 Kings 3:5-9). God approved Solomon's request by making him world-renowned for his wisdom and granting him wealth and honor as well.

It took seven years for Solomon to have the temple built, and he held a fourteen-day festival of dedication for it, sacrificing 22,000 cattle and 120,000 sheep and goats in fellowship offerings to the Lord. Then God appeared to Solomon in a dream again, affirming the consecration of the temple and reminding Solomon of his personal responsibility to be "pure in heart and action" (MSG).

As God's "chosen people, a royal priesthood" (1 Peter 2:4-9), we have everything going for us—"every spiritual blessing in Christ" including "wisdom and understanding" (Ephesians 1:3-8). We are commissioned to be "living stones" in God's worldwide church. As God did with Solomon, Jesus encourages us to ask for "whatever" (see John 15:16).

Maybe like Solomon we've asked for wisdom. Maybe we've worked hard to build a church and gone all out in public worship celebrations. Now God reminds us about personal integrity. May we learn from Solomon's sorry example not to let success go to our heads.

God of all discernment and wisdom, we praise and thank You for blessing us and granting success in our endeavors. Holy Spirit, keep us humble and faithful.

Suffering and Integrity - 1

"...till I die, I will not deny my integrity...."

—Job 27:5

JOB IS FAMOUS for his patience, but he spoke with plenty of impatience toward God for his suffering and in response to his friends' judgmental reasoning. Super-human patience is not what God required, and Job knew it. He felt free to voice his complaints and curse the day of his birth.

What God commended about Job was his integrity (2:3). In spite of his wife's urging, "Curse God and die! ...Job did not sin in what he said" (2:9, 10). And in spite of his friends' loquacious attempts to persuade him that his suffering could be God's just punishment for wrong-doing, Job stubbornly believed that God would ultimately vindicate his integrity: "I will maintain my innocence and never let go of it; my conscience will not reproach me as long as I live" (27:6).

Job knew his heart was right with God. He was not claiming to be sinless, but desired to know his offenses, repent and be forgiven of them (7:21 and 10:2). Job's persistent faith and integrity reached for Jesus with prophetic inspiration: "I know that my redeemer lives, and that in the end he will stand on the earth. And after my skin has been destroyed, yet in my flesh I will see God" (19:25, 26).

Holy Spirit, mold us to be persons of integrity. Lord Jesus, our Redeemer, we praise You.

Suffering and Integrity - 2

Read Psalm 41.

> "In my integrity you uphold me and set me in your presence forever."
>
> **—Psalm 41:12**

KING DAVID PRAYED this Psalm when he was weakened and alienated by illness, which could have been due to guilt and stress, exacerbated by old age. "Have mercy on me, Lord; heal me, for I have sinned against you," he confesses (4). Like Jesus, David's "close friend" betrayed him (9). Like Job, he clung to his integrity and appealed to God for mercy. At a time when his life was falling apart, David knew that only the one who had knit him together in his mother's womb could put him together again for good.

In a prayer letter, I read about an African Christian woman who prayed this Psalm when she lost her teaching job due to parents finding out she was HIV-positive after a hospital blood transfusion. She kept praying and continued to be welcomed and supported in her church fellowship. Two years later she died of AIDS. Now she is established in God's majestic presence forever.

The root meaning of integrity is wholeness. No matter how sick or broken we are, no matter how mistreated and maligned, in Jesus we are upright in character, our souls are completely well.

Lord of all life and goodness, we praise and thank You for Your royal treatment.

Duplicity and Integrity

"The integrity of the upright guides them, but the unfaithful are destroyed by their duplicity."

—Proverbs 11:3

MEDITATING ON THIS wise precept and related proverbs, I imagine an announcement in the Holy Spirit's newsletter to all churches.

HELP WANTED: People of integrity to serve as Twelve-Step sponsors, mentors, teachers, counselors, small and large group leaders, foster parents, big brothers and sisters, lawyers, city-planners, recreation directors, social workers and more.

Requirements: Honesty, trustworthiness, confidentiality, ability to let your conscience be your guide, internal yet unselfish motivation. No double standards or hypocrisy.

Benefits: twenty-four-hour security (Proverbs 10:9 and 13:6); peace of mind; the joy of reflecting God's love in faithful service to people.

Schools try to teach children and teenagers character traits that will add up to integrity. A company called "Integrity Services" offers "integrity coaching" to help organizations "get and keep customers." Politicians known for their integrity have the highest approval ratings. Yet popular movies and television shows often portray people who are upright as *uptight*. It is hip to "go with the flow" and follow the crowd rather than develop good habits and live by biblical principles.

Lord of integrity, guide us by Your goodness. Deliver us from mixed messages. Bless our lives and work.

Truth and Integrity

> "By myself I have sworn, my mouth has uttered in all integrity a word that will not be revoked: Before me every knee will bow...."
>
> —Isaiah 45:23

WE SWEAR IN court to "tell the truth, the whole truth, and nothing but the truth." The oath affirms the integrity of our testimony. Swearing "so help me God" can be a sincere prayer as we realize the frailty of our integrity. Fears, ego, prejudice and selective memory keep confusing us as we speak. When an elected official takes the oath of office, he or she needs to humbly appeal to God as well.

God is the only source of and standard for integrity. Only God can swear by himself. Only God can absolutely guarantee that his promises and plans will be fulfilled. God has perfect memory, perfect foresight and no bias. God not only knows everything that happened in the past, but knows everything everyone was and is thinking and everything that will happen in the future.

God would be as incomprehensible and frightening to us as the size of the universe or the force of a tornado if not for Jesus who showed us that God is the source of all love.

Integrity is based on love. It is the perfect union of truth and love. God's promise that all people will worship Christ the Lord (Philippians 2:9-11) is completely reliable *and* the best, most wonderful, joyful, peaceful, loving fulfillment of creation's promise. Then finally we will each and all shine with pure integrity, reflecting the one in whose image we were made.

Lord, let every part of my mind, every word I speak affirm Your truth and love.

Influence and Integrity - 1

"Teacher, we know that you are a man of integrity. You aren't swayed by others, because you pay no attention to who they are; but you teach the way of God in accordance with the truth."

—Mark 12:14

EACH YEAR OUTSTANDING teachers in our state receive the Governor's Citation for "demonstration of high integrity and ability meriting our great trust and respect." Surely the recipients, and hopefully *all* teachers, avoid playing favorites or discriminating against students on any basis.

Jesus was known for his integrity and impartiality in a time and place where these godly traits were rare. But there were plenty of proud, hypocritical and jealous leaders. A group of them sent some Pharisees and Herodians to put Jesus' in a double bind with a tax question cleverly designed to crack his integrity. If he said yes, people should pay the imperial tax, the Pharisees figured they could turn Jewish people against Jesus for condoning Rome's cruel occupation; if he said no to this tax, they figured the Herodians would have him arrested for treason.

Jesus' wise answer, "Give back to Caesar what is Caesar's and to God what is God's" amazed them. Jesus had exposed their lack of integrity. The image on the coin was of the emperor, and the inscription would have said "Tiberias Caesar Augustus, son of the divine Augustus" (NIV footnote Matthew 22:19). His answer rebuked the Herodians for emperor worship and rebuked the Pharisees for not giving themselves, made in the image of God, to God.

Thank You, holy God, for teachers and leaders who show Your integrity and wisdom.

Influence and Integrity - 2

"In your teaching show integrity, seriousness and soundness of speech that cannot be condemned...."

—Titus 2:7b, 8

O N A PBS radio talk show yesterday, I heard bank officers and university officials defending "the integrity of the student loan process." They insisted that every effort was being made to ensure that advice was not "tainted" by conflict of interest and that there were no kickbacks or "sweetheart deals" as they strive for an "unambiguous atmosphere of integrity." The big words sounded flippant and fake—especially in the light of survey data and student interviews.

The apostle Paul advises Titus to teach, witness or speak with clear integrity befitting the grave import of his message in order that no facts or opinions will contradict what he says. Church leaders are to back up what they say with "blameless" lives (Titus 1: 6, 7); "in everything" Titus is to "set them an example by doing what is good" (2:7a).

I do not profess to be a teacher and probably will never speak on the radio, but I am beginning to realize that I do teach or testify in all of my communications and interactions. This insight helps me pray more and talk less.

Holy Spirit, purify my life and words that I may honor you in all I say and do.

Strong Joy

Read Nehemiah 8.

> "Go and enjoy choice food and sweet drinks, and send some to those who have nothing prepared. This day is holy to our Lord. Do not grieve, for the joy of the Lord is your strength."
> —Nehemiah 8:10

THAT LAST LINE, personalized by a spirited songwriter, sings in my mind. It's the title and first line of a Scripture song, repeated three more times in the first verse and at the end of the other three verses, linking joy to praise, living water and healing of broken hearts.

But now I want to let go of the tune and reflect on Nehemiah's words to the crowd of men, women and children listening to Ezra reading and the Levites explaining holy Scripture. What impresses me first is that "all the people had been weeping as they listened to the words of the Law" (9). Were they gripped by conviction of sin? Does God's holy Word ever move me to tears?

Secondly, the instructions for celebration not only include enjoying "choice food and sweet drinks," but also providing for "those who have nothing prepared"—sharing with the poor. How can we include others in our church festivities and refreshments to spread the joy of the Lord? The joy is not something we drum up; it's God's gift, a fruit of God's Spirit that is multiplied by love. "And on that day they offered great sacrifices, rejoicing because God had given them great joy" (Nehemiah 12:43).

Finally, because the joy is from God, who is love, who always forgives, always provides and protects, it is our stronghold, our inner fortress against all despair and fear. That's worth celebrating, and the Israelites did—for a week! "And their joy was very great" (17).

Lord God, we praise You for the gift of strong, solid joy. Help us to celebrate as Your forgiven and loving people.

Heart Joy

"The precepts of the Lord are right, giving joy to the heart."
—Psalm 19:8

FORTUNATELY, I AM not trying to change your perception of anything, or we would have a battle of who's right, and I'm not concerned with being right," my daughter wrote in reply to my email questioning her beliefs. In our phone conversation several days later, I expressed concern for her lack of joy in living. How foolish of me to put her on the defensive, only showing the weakness of my own joy! "All my friends know I am a very joyful person," she exclaimed.

God's precepts are summed up in love—loving God above all and our neighbor as ourselves. Although my daughter does not find joy in keeping certain commandments as traditionally interpreted, it is not for me to say that she is not joyful and her happiness is superficial. I need to be careful not to project my sadness about her lifestyle onto her. I don't want to judge her for seeing my concern with "being right" as unloving.

How do the Lord's precepts, God's "life-maps" (MSG) show the way to joy, "rejoicing the heart" (NKJV)? In millions of surprising or unremarkable ways for different people at different times. For me, this heart joy beams even as I struggle to communicate the truth of God's Word, seeing glimmers of Jesus' love transform my "clanging cymbals" into faithful testimonies.

Holy Spirit, keep Your unconditional love and true joy flowing through our hearts and lives.

Resounding Joy

Read Psalm 100.

> "Shout for joy to the Lord, all the earth. Worship the Lord with gladness; come before him with joyful songs."
> —**Psalm 100:1-2**

SPARROWS CHIRPED, ROBINS sang, cardinals whistled outside our windows. The Holy Spirit called me to joy at 6 AM Sunday morning, impressing the opening verses of Psalm 100 on my mind. An hour later, after our walk by the lake, my husband and I read these joyful words. I remember rejoicing as the TODAY devotional recalled me to joy.

God's Word, echoed by all creation, calls us to joyous worship in the power of the Spirit. We were created and are being rejuvenated to give praise, shout loud hosannas, pour out joyful gratitude in all kinds of creative ways.

In church that morning our hearts shouted gladly in tune with Hanna's trumpet, Christoff's saxophone and Jaelyn's clarinet. We made a joyful noise, sometimes even on key, as the choir's descant soared. "For the Lord is good and his love endures forever; his faithfulness continues through all generations" (5).

Thank You, Lord, for letting us know You are God, You made us and we are Your people. Thanks for the way all creation reverberates in praise to You. Thanks for the joys of musical worship.

Heavenly Joy

"They will enter Zion with singing; everlasting joy will crown their heads. Gladness and joy will overtake them, and sorrow and sighing will flee away."

—Isaiah 35:10

IN TIMES OF war, injustice and persecution, God's people today, like those in Isaiah's day, rejoice in the prophet's vision of unending pure joy. Isaiah's prophecies shine with justice, peace and joy in the holy city on the new earth. Konstantin Zhigulin, a young Russian composer featured in *RADIX* magazine (33:1), caught echoes of that joy in his suite for chamber choir and orchestra titled "Let There Be Joy" based on the book of Isaiah.

Also in that issue of *RADIX* there is a story of holy joy in a crowded makeshift recording studio in Darfur. Frank Fortunato of Heart Sounds International "imagined angels reserving front-row seats...for vigorous Dinka worship around the Throne" as the eighteen-member choir of "suffering Sudanese believers made us homesick for heaven."

Those of us who have not experienced a lot of sorrow and sighing in our own lives need to be in solidarity with brothers and sisters in Christ whose health and welfare is threatened daily. Personal contact and identification with needy churches and individuals in other countries or cultures will enable us to identify with Israel and Judah in the Bible. Then our songs of joy will be sincere as we anticipate the glorious music of the new Jerusalem.

Show me ways, Lord, to walk and sing with Your suffering people until Your kingdom of joy comes on earth as it is in heaven.

Jesus' Joy

"I say these things while I am still in the world, so that they may have the full measure of my joy within them."

—John 17:13

NO HUMAN BEING ever knows suffering and sorrow as Jesus does. None of us know or could bear to know every evil, every hurt, or every pain that every person who ever lives ever inflicts or endures. Jesus knows and cares. No wonder he is called "the man of sorrows." No wonder artists depict his face in anguish or sadness.

And yet the day before Jesus' crucifixion he speaks twice of his joy. First he teaches his disciples about divine, compassionate, sacrificial love, "so that my joy may be in you and that your joy may be complete" (John 15:9-17). Then he prays for believers: "Holy Father, protect them by the power of your name, the name you gave me, so that they may be one as we are one. I am coming to you now, but I say these things while I am still in the world, so that they may have the full measure of my joy within them" (John 17:11-13).

The secret of Jesus' joy is devoted love. John the Baptist testified about the joy his love for Jesus gave: "The bride belongs to the bridegroom. The friend who attends the bridegroom waits and listens for him, and is full of joy when he hears the bridegroom's voice. That joy is mine, and it is now complete" (John 3:29).

Jesus calls us his friends. He calls the church his bride. We belong to him. He is always praying for us. His Holy Spirit with ever-growing love, joy and peace is ours for the asking. "Ask and you will receive, and your joy will be complete" (John 16:24).

Dearest Jesus, we rejoice in Your love which enables us to live and love joyfully.

Cultivating Joy

"Rejoice in the Lord always. I will say it again: Rejoice!"
—Philippians 4:4

WITH IMPERATIVE EXCLAMATIONS, Paul, the great teacher, missionary and church planter, urges Philippian believers to enjoy God and each other (see also 3:1). With repeated superlatives he emphasizes joy in grateful prayer for brothers and sisters in Christ: "I thank my God *every* time I remember you. In *all* my prayers for *all* of you, I *always* pray with joy because of your partnership in the gospel..." (1:3-5 italics mine).

Christians, of all people, can radiate what the French call *joie de vivre*—zest for life—keen, buoyant, hearty or carefree enjoyment of life. We are glad to get up in the morning. We say with enthusiasm: "This is the day the Lord has made; let us rejoice and be glad in it" (Psalm 118:24). Rejoicing in God's loving presence is like taking a daily Spirit shower or bath.

Joy is a fruit of the Spirit, but we need to cultivate it. That's why Paul kept writing about his own joy and telling Christians to be joyful. Paul rejoiced that Christ was being preached "whether from false motives or true" (1:18). He rejoiced in prison, confident of vindication "through your prayers and God's provision of the Spirit" (1:19). He counseled unity and humility in the church which would "make my joy complete" (2:2, 3). Christian community is the primary means of cultivating joy: "I am glad and rejoice with all of you. So you too should be glad and rejoice with me" (2:18). Paul even calls the church family at Philippi his "joy and crown" (4:1).

All of the fruits of the Spirit are of the love species. As we grow in love for God, the soil of our hearts is receptive to the Holy Spirit's plantings of love for other people. Soon these love shoots produce joy, peace, patience, kindness, goodness, faithfulness, gentleness and self-control (Galatians 5:22, 23).

Thank You for joy, Holy Spirit. Teach me to rejoice greatly in You today, Lord Jesus.

Believing Joy

"Though you have not seen him, you love him; and even though you do not see him now, you believe in him and are filled with an inexpressible and glorious joy...."

—1 Peter 1:8

JOY IS TOO big for words. Maybe that's why clowns are often silent. Their smiles, loving attitudes, and actions shine with joy. Many churches and Christian groups minister humbly and joyfully to people of all ages through clowning.

The chorus of a hymn written by B.E. Warren is based on the King James Version of today's verse: "It is joy unspeakable and full of glory. Oh, the half has never yet been told!"

Some may say Christian joy is inexpressible because Jesus is invisible. But as Jesus told Thomas: "Blessed and happy and to be envied are those who have never seen Me, and yet have believed and adhered to and trusted in and relied on Me" (John 20:29—AB).

Others may say our joy is unspeakable because Jesus tells us to rejoice when we're persecuted (Matthew 5:10-12). But we can trust him. Those like Peter who did see him and were persecuted have been inspired by the Holy Spirit to express the inexpressible. The same Holy Spirit ignites wondrous joy in us as we believe and act on God's Word in love.

Glory is inexpressible too, but glorious joy in hope, faith and love is hard to hide. Thank God for believing poets, singers, clowns and artists who believe in Jesus. They give us glimpses.

Lord Jesus, we love You. We praise You for huge, quiet, unending joy.

Safe-keeping

Read Numbers 6:22 – 27.

"The Lord bless you and keep you...."

—Numbers 6:24

YESTERDAY I READ a yellow ribbon bumper sticker which expressed a mother's prayer: "Please keep my son safe." Only God can truly keep us safe, whether we are at war, walking to the store, or battling traffic on the beltway.

God told Moses to tell Aaron and his sons: "put my name on the Israelites, and I will bless them" (27). Pastors and priests today raise their hands and offer this benediction, these good words from God to congregations throughout the world.

How is the message received? It depends on the hearts of the hearers. Those who know how needy they are, how dependent on God for all goodness and protection like the Israelites were, long to hear and receive God's promise week after week.

One meaning of the Hebrew word for keep is "to hedge about, as with thorns." I picture the thorns on the outside and beautiful roses on the inside. God promises to keep us safe, surrounding his people with a living wall of protection. Every time we leave the gathering of believers or God's "sanctuary" it is good for us to be reminded: "The Lord will keep you from all harm—he will watch over your life" (Psalm 121:7). In Jesus who wore the crown of thorns our life is secure.

Thank You, Lord. Teach us to be aware of and to share Your continuous blessings and constant safekeeping.

Sabbath-keeping

"Observe the Sabbath day by keeping it holy."
—Deuteronomy 5:12

SABBATH MEANS REST. Our loving creator knew we would need one day in seven to rest, but that we would not realize this on our own. God revealed it to us first in the creation story: "God blessed the seventh day and made it holy, because on it he rested from all the work of creating that he had done" (Genesis 2:3). Second, in giving the covenant rules at Sinai, God made Sabbath-keeping "a sign between me and you for the generations to come, so you may know that I am the Lord, who makes you holy" (Exodus 31:13).

The prophets later warned of God's punishments for desecrating the Sabbath. Desecration is the opposite of consecration. To desecrate is to defile or profane, to abuse the sacredness of something holy. The Jews came up with precise rules defining desecration of the day of rest, such as carrying loads or walking more than a certain distance.

Because of Jesus we know that the Sabbath is a gift, "made for people, not people for the Sabbath" (Mark 2:27). We can't *make* the Sabbath holy any more than we can make ourselves holy. God does that. All we need to do is receive the gift humbly and gratefully, observe it, *keep* it holy by worshiping the giver and Lord of the Sabbath. Respect the gift by honoring the giver.

Rather than judging people for Sabbath desecration, we can relax, admire God's creation as he did, celebrate new life in Christ, enjoy each other's company, and praise God. We can keep on "meeting together...encouraging one another—and all the more as...the Day" that will begin the eternal Sabbath approaches (Hebrews 10:25).

Lord, help us to stop rushing around carrying loads of self-righteousness or guilt. Let us rest in Your holiness.

Covenant-keeping

"...he is the faithful God, keeping his covenant of love to a thousand generations of those who love him and keep his commandments."

—Deuteronomy 7:9

KEEP THE BALL rolling" originated with a game called bandy in which players tried to keep the bandy ball moving toward the opponent's goal. In the 1840 presidential campaign, candidates' supporters kept huge balls covered with slogans rolling for hundreds of miles in the race for the White House.

To keep the ball rolling for the long haul, we need encouragement. We hear this every day. Stressed workers say they can barely keep their heads above water. A tired caregiver says, "I don't know how long I can keep this up." A teacher tells her student to "keep up the good work." A boss hollers "Keep on truckin'." A church sign urges "Keep the faith, baby!"

Love is for keeps. God is the only sure keeper, the one who keeps us going, keeps us faithful. God always keeps his promises, keeps on loving us, no matter what. Our willpower won't keep us on track. Only by knowing and loving God can we keep his law of love. Then in the Holy Spirit's power we will "keep on keeping on." Our children's children will see God's Word not merely as a family keepsake, for our lives will validate its truths in faithful love.

Faithful Father God, we love You. Thanks for keeping Your people faithful over hundreds of generations already.

Peace-keeping

"You will keep in perfect peace those whose minds are steadfast, because they trust in you."

—Isaiah 26:3

THIS PROFESSION OF faith is addressed to God the Holy Spirit, source of the inner peace from which all outer peace arises. It is part of a song of praise which Isaiah prophesies will be sung by God's restored people. Many whose relationship to God has been restored by faith in Jesus keep claiming its promise.

Peter was one who experienced this amazing peace, at least briefly, as he walked on water, not sinking until his trust wavered when he took his eyes and mind off Jesus.

Keeping focused is not easy. Our attention spans are short. Our mature, analytic minds squelch childlike trust. We suspect that one-track minds are feeble, blind or obsessive. Richard Foster in his book, *Prayer: Finding the Heart's True Home,* writes that "while this 'practice of the presence of God' is strenuous, everything else ceases to be so."

It takes discipline to develop a steady, trusting mind. Different disciplines work for different people; some of the basic ones are solitude, silence, Sabbath, prayer, meditation, Bible study, journaling and fasting. The rewards of being kept in God's complete *shalom* far outweigh the efforts of keeping faithful in disciplines.

Holy Prince of Peace, we want to trust You more. Keep our minds and hearts set on You.

Keepers Lose, Losers Keep

Read Luke 17:20-37.

> "Whoever tries to keep their life will lose it, and whoever loses their life will preserve it."
>
> —Luke 17:33

LIFE DOESN'T KEEP. Everybody (every *body*) has an expiration date. And yet no matter how old we are, we find it difficult to accept that life is ebbing away and will end in death. We keep trying to liven up or extend our lives with TV, movie and internet screens, new clothes, beauticians, sports, travel, diets, fitness classes, doctors and medications.

Jesus tells his disciples: "If you grasp and cling to life on your terms, you'll lose it, but if you let that life go, you'll get life on God's terms" (MSG). The gospel writers repeat Jesus' "keepers losers, losers keepers" paradox seven times in slightly different forms, emphasizing its importance.

Members of faith communities in the tradition of Church of the Savior in Washington DC make a yearly resolution which begins: "I unreservedly and with abandon commit my life and destiny to Christ..." That sense of abandon and unreserved commitment goes against our life-clutching instincts and seems reckless. We want to "get a life" but not lose the life we have.

Only by yielding control can we preserve our lives. As we keep on losing ourselves to Christ, we begin to experience abundant, eternal love-filled life in his Spirit. Lot's wife and the barn-building man in Jesus' parable tried to keep their lives but lost them. In contrast, Abram and the woman who anointed Jesus' feet with expensive perfume were willing to lose their lives and had them well-preserved.

Lord Jesus, forgive my clutching possessions, achievements, knowledge, time or money as if they were my life or could extend my life. Thank You for being my daily and eternal life preserver.

Heavenly Book-keeping

Read 1 Peter 1:3-12.

"This inheritance is kept in heaven for you...."

—1 Peter 1:4-5

THE GREY-HAIRED WOMAN was homeless, penniless and to most people nameless. Yet as she stood in line at Miriam's Kitchen, Georgia beamed confidently, greeting everyone: "Good morning, Joe, how's your leg? Pedro, it's good to see you! God bless you, MaryAnn. May I sit with you today, George?"

Serving fruit salad at the breakfast counter, I wondered what Georgia's secret was? How could she be so carefree, joyful and caring? I overheard her saying something to John about a reservation. "No, you don't need reservations for these meals," I said. Georgia laughed, as John told me, "She was talking about her everlasting Kingdom-come timeshare reservation."

"What in the world?" I mused. Georgia looked back over her shoulder, exclaiming, "It's out of this world, and the same one who keeps an eye on me and you every day and keeps us happy is keeping our places reserved!"

That night I thanked God for Georgia, marveling at the interest her inheritance must be accruing as she daily lays up treasures in heaven. Since then I appreciate my own inheritance more, realizing that apart from Jesus, I would ultimately be homeless, helpless and nameless.

Thank You, Father, for adopting us because of Jesus and not keeping our inheritance a secret.

Inkeep and Upkeep

Read Jude 17-25.

> "...keep yourselves in God's love...."
>
> —Jude 21

> "To him who is able to keep you from stumbling...."
>
> —Jude 24

KEEPING OUR MARRIAGE vows is a three-way commitment between God, my husband and me. But God deserves all the credit for our faithfulness and growth in love. We only need to keep ourselves in God's love, our spirits responsive to God's tending and molding. God never drops us, always holds us up and together, keeps us from stumbling, slipping or falling.

Church membership is also a three-way commitment—between Jesus, each member, and the rest of the congregation. And as in marriage, so in the church, God the Holy Spirit keeps us vibrant and faithful while we remain in God's love.

Each member, each couple or family, and each church community has various ways of "staying right at the center of God's love… arms open and outstretched, ready for the mercy of our Master, Jesus Christ" (MSG). My husband and I enjoy praying and reading aloud together daily, as well as celebrating God's love in weekly worship services with the family of believers. This summer at our church new staff and members are welcoming children, teens and other neighbors to "Thursday Nights Live." There will be plenty of food, fun, fellowship and creative expression centered in the home-written musical, "New Moves."

Lord God, we praise You for Your love. Forgive us when we forget You and think we can manage on our own. Thank You for keeping us strong as we live and worship together.

Martial Love

"Love and faithfulness keep a king safe; through love his throne is made secure."

—Proverbs 20:28

WHAT WAS SOLOMON thinking? What does love have to do with homeland security? And what does this proverb say to people all over the world today?

Although in the end Solomon failed to practice what he preached, his words flowed from God's wisdom and personal experience. He knew that his loving, reliable and practically demonstrated devotion to his people would ensure their loyalty to him.

Chesed, the Hebrew word for love used in this proverb, can be translated as mercy, kindness or loving-kindness. It was one of the primary characteristics of God as he revealed himself to his covenant people. The king, as God's representative, was honored and protected by the people to the degree that he showed this godly love.

Once I heard a sermon about each of us in a sense being a king or queen, having a sphere of influence which includes people for whom we are given responsibility. In a democracy each of us exerts our kingdom authority as we speak out on issues and support candidates. What motivates our voting? Fear, selfishness or love? Can leaders in democracies and the United Nations show love and faithfulness to those who suffer under unsafe, unjust regimes?

King of all kings, we praise You for the everlasting security of Your faithful love.

Marital Love

"Many waters cannot quench love; rivers cannot sweep it away. If one were to give all the wealth of one's house for love, it would be utterly scorned."

—Song of Songs 8:7

THE SONG OF Songs is a dialog of passionate love poems between a bride and her husband. The woman speaks first, more often, and last. She exalts "marital love as the strongest, most … invincible force in human experience" (NIV Study Bible footnote). In her time and place raging flood waters represented the terror of primeval chaos. She asserts love's infinitely priceless value: "Love can't be bought, love can't be sold—it's not to be found in the marketplace" (MSG).

True love prevails against all threats, fears and dangers, tangible or intangible. In Christian marriage we vow: "For better, for worse, for richer, for poorer, in sickness and in health, to love and to cherish until we are parted by death."

Song of Songs sings to our fearful, drifting, market-dazed souls. It inspires a couple's respect for and enjoyment of each other's sexuality, companionship and loyalty. By its inclusion in Holy Scriptures, along with the New Testament metaphor of the Church as the bride of Christ, the Song affirms marital love as God's gift, exactly what he knew would fulfill us when God created us in his image—male and female (Genesis 1:27).

Loving Master, thank You for lifelong love. Please strengthen and enrich our marriages.

Triple-true Love

"'Love the Lord your God with all your heart and with all your soul and with all your mind.' This is the first and greatest commandment."

—Matthew 22:37

JESUS QUOTES FROM Deuteronomy, the premier Jewish law book in answer to the law expert's question, "which is the greatest commandment in the Law?" He quotes from the *Shema* (Hebrew word for hear), which begins, "Hear, O Israel: The Lord our God, the Lord is one" (Deuteronomy 6:4). The *Shema* was to be taught to every child, discussed everywhere, posted on every doorway, and even printed on tiny scrolls put in pouches called phylacteries, strapped on wrists and foreheads. Jesus exposed the hypocrisy of law teachers and Pharisees who "make their phylacteries wide" not because they love God, but "for people to see" (Matthew 23:5).

It's easy for us to condemn the Pharisees for their attempts to show themselves superior to everyone including Jesus. But who can go all out in loving God? Who has ever loved God fully? Only Jesus who is himself God. Only God who is love in action—for, with and in us—can by his Holy Spirit motivate and energize us to love God with all our "passion and prayer and intelligence" (MSG). Just as the holy trinity is one God, so we must be balanced and unified in loving God, emotionally, spiritually, mentally, and yes, even physically—"with all your heart and with all your soul and with all your strength" (Deuteronomy 6:5).

Lord God, to know You is to love You. Thank You for revealing Yourself to us in Jesus. Keep us from pretense, pride and half-hearted love.

Love Who?

Read Luke 6:27-36.

> "Love your enemies, do good to those who hate you, bless those who curse you, pray for those who mistreat you."
>
> —Luke 6:27-28

MOST OF US don't realize we have enemies. We are sheltered from hate crimes. Yet we are quick to complain or protest at the slightest hint of mistreatment. Loving and praying for those who don't treat us right is contrary to human nature. We can't even imagine loving enemies.

But Jesus did. Jesus knew that hatred in response to hatred multiplies hatred; but love in response to hatred can overcome hatred as the hater sees the possibility of love. The highest expression of love for enemies is forgiveness. Stephen, the first Christian martyr, like Jesus, prayed for his killers as he died: "Lord, do not hold this sin against them" (Acts 7:60).

Perhaps while the young man at Virginia Tech was shooting, some of his thirty-two victims were praying for and forgiving him. Certainly some victims' family members forgave him and showed love to his family afterward. Thousands, maybe millions, have been moved by Corrie Ten Boom's story of forgiving the guard at the Nazi concentration camp. In 2006, Immaculee Ilibagiza published her story, *Left to Tell: Discovering God Amidst the Rwandan Holocaust.* God's love kept her praying and believing as she faced killers repeatedly and enabled her to forgive her family's killer. Evangelicals for Social Action's Epistle announced the "Adopt a Terrorist for Prayer" signup this week. Could that be a first step for us?

Lord Jesus, we praise You for Your life and death in perfect love. Thank You for Your empowerment to keep praying, forgiving and loving even enemies.

Love's Descendants

Read 1 Corinthians 13.

"Love is patient. Love is kind."

—1 Corinthians 13:4

LOVE IS THE mother of all the fruits of the Spirit. Sometimes one fruit gives birth to another, and love is the joyful grandmother.

Many loving surrogate mothers have nourished my spirit with God's joyful, peaceful love. Accompanying Edwina, Ismay, Corrine and others to church, seniors' activities or doctor appointments has tilled my heart soil for God's seeds of patience. The more time I spend with each mother, especially alone in the car, the more I enjoy their company as I grow in love for them. From this patient, listening love, kindness sprouts in appreciative actions—hospice visits, birthday celebrations, phone calls, meals with friends.

The Bible version which these mothers grew up with says "love suffers long." Patience is love's tenacious, enduring ability to keep trusting, keep hoping, keep persevering in love for God and people, no matter what. The Greek word for kind means to show oneself useful, act benevolently or beneficially. Godly patience is a wonderful seedbed for kindness, planted and watered by love.

God of all loving patience and kindness, thank You for mothers, grandmothers and so many others who nurture Your fruitful love in us.

God is Love

Read 1 John 3:11-18 and 4:7-21.

"Dear friends, let us love one another, for love comes from God"

—1 John 4:7

NO WORD EXPLORATION in the Bible is more mysterious and wonderful than love. No book is more universally appealing and eternally revealing of love than the Bible.

The apostle John, who identifies himself as "the disciple whom Jesus loved," reveals God's love in his eyewitness account of Jesus, known as the gospel of John. In his first epistle to scattered believers, John uses forms of the word love forty-six times. His own loving attitude is shown by forty-one personal or familial forms of address and ways of referring to people. The most common of these are "dear children" or "dear friends," "children of God," "fellowship" or "fellow believer," and "one another."

The peak of all this love talk comes in chapter four, where John proclaims first: "Whoever does not love does not know God, because God is love" (4:8); and secondly, "God is love. Whoever lives in love lives in God, and God in them" (4:16).

Fortunately John comes out of these ethereal love clouds in his epistle as in the gospel. Otherwise we might draw the conclusion that God is only love, or any kind of love, or that love is God. "This is how we know what love is: Jesus Christ laid down his life for us. And we ought to lay down our lives for one another. If any one of you has material possessions and sees a brother or sister in need but has no pity on them, how can the love of God be in you" (3:16, 17)?

Holy Spirit of God, keep us in God's love as we pour ourselves out in love for others. May everyone know we are Christians by our love.

Loving Care

Read Revelation 3:14-22.

"Those whom I love I rebuke and discipline."
—**Revelation 3:19**

GOOD PARENTS KNOW that love for children must include discipline and occasional reproof. But most of us are either too lax or too harsh. Based on our own childhood experiences, some of us may associate discipline with abuse or manipulation rather than with love; others who were neglected or "spoiled rotten" as children, may overcompensate to the other extreme with their own children.

After raising nine children in their inner city Baltimore home, Jim and Lyla Dupree knew the need for loving discipline. For the past twenty years their "Do You Know Where Your Children Are?" program has creatively ministered to hundreds of middle school children and their parents with accountability incentives and face-to-face home contact.

The apostle John's letter, dictated by Master Jesus to the church at Laodicea, expresses strong disapproval of their lukewarm, self-satisfied Christianity. Thankfully, God's love always includes appropriate discipline, both of individuals and churches. God always knows where his children are. Jesus' message to us today is the same as to the Laodiceans: "The people I love, I call to account—prod and correct and guide so that they'll live at their best" (MSG).

Thank You Father for Your love that keeps us on track. Jesus, we hear You knocking on our heart's door. We want to open it and welcome You to come in and sit down for a meal with us.

Blessed by the Maker

Read Genesis 12:1-5.

> **"I will make you into a great nation, and I will bless you; I will make your name great, and you will be a blessing."**
> **—Genesis 12:2**

AT AGE SEVETY-FIVE, Abram and his wife Sarai were nobodies with no children, whom God called to be nomads. What they had going for them was their loyalty to God their Maker and to each other. Somehow Abram heard God's call and promise: "Go…to the land I will show you" and decided to follow God's instructions.

All of us forget our Maker at times and try to make it on our own. Abram and Sarai were no exception. Yet as their own efforts got them into trouble, God reminded them that he was not only the creator of their individual bodies and lives, but the one who created all the stars and who would initiate his worldwide kingdom of blessing through them.

Now that Jesus has come, God's great trans-national nation of faithful people is spreading throughout the earth. The Maker keeps calling nobodies of all ages. We gaze at starry skies like Abram and like the Magi, and his promises resound. As the stars are countless, new ones yet being formed and discovered, so are God's blessings through Christ Jesus.

Heavenly nation-builder we praise You. Thank You Father for making us Your children, making our name great, making us a blessing in Jesus.

Inspired by the Maker

"See that you make them according to the pattern shown you on the mountain."

—Exodus 25:40

THE MOUNTAIN WAS a place of transcendent mystery where Moses glimpsed God's glory. On the mountain God also instructed Moses to have his people build and furnish the tabernacle to "make a sanctuary for me, and I will dwell among them" (Exodus 25:8).

God designated Bezalel, filling him "with wisdom, with understanding, with knowledge and with all kinds of skills—to make artistic designs for work in gold, silver and bronze, to cut and set stones, to work in wood, and to engage in all kinds of crafts." God appointed Oholiab to assist Bezalel and gave "ability to all the skilled workers to make everything" he commanded for the tent of meeting and its furnishings (Exodus 31:1-11).

No graven images, no golden calves—but art and architecture can facilitate and enhance worship. Icons need not be idols. Creativity in visual arts is one of our Maker's wondrous gifts to us who are made in his image. Art's glorious origin and purpose are God inspired. As the master artist of all creation, God continually shows us his transcendent pattern for excellence, when and wherever our eyes are open to behold.

Maker of heaven and earth, we praise You. Thank You for inspiring us to make things that reflect the beauty of Your creation and express our individual creativity.

God the Peace-maker

Read Psalm 46.

> "He makes wars cease to the ends of the earth."
>
> **—Psalm 46:9**

WHO WILL BE the history makers, its movers and shakers? Not terrorists; not even those who make war on terrorists. Jesus said, "Blessed are the peacemakers, for they will be called children of God" (Matthew 5:9). I pray that Christians and churches follow Jesus, the prince of peace, and take the lead in bringing ends to conflicts throughout the world.

Jesus also said, "All authority in heaven and on earth has been given to me. Therefore go and make disciples of all nations..." (Matthew 28:18, 19). Sadly, for many years Christians tried to spread Christianity with the sword. And far too many churches today are filled with war-makers. How many more true disciples can be made using the Spirit's nonviolent, creative, loving, peaceful means!

With Francis of Assisi I pray to be used with my sisters and brothers in Christ as channels of God's peace, forgiveness, hope and joy. I dream of the day when peace memorials will replace war memorials, when nations will "beat their swords into plowshares and their spears into pruning hooks. Nation will not take up sword against nation, nor will they train for war anymore" (Isaiah 2:4).

Lord Jesus, You are our Peace. Thank You for the promise of an end to war. Mobilize us to follow You faithfully in peace-making.

Maker of All Creatures

Read Psalm 104.

> **"How many are your works, Lord! In wisdom you made them all; the earth is full of your creatures."**
>
> **—Psalm 104:24**

THE UNNAMED AUTHOR of Psalm 104 traces God's involvement with everything he made: "The Lord wraps himself in light" (2); "He makes the clouds his chariot" (3); "He makes winds his messengers" (4); "He makes springs pour water" (10); "He makes grass grow for the cattle, and plants for people to cultivate" (14).

The psalmist marvels at the numbers and kinds of animals God made. He lists beasts of the field, birds of the sky, beasts of the forest, and "the sea, vast and spacious, teeming with creatures beyond number" (25). His creation hymn specifically celebrates God's provision for wild donkeys, cattle, storks, mountain goats, hyrax (rock badger or coney), lions and "the leviathan, which you formed to frolic there" (26)—sounds like a whale to me!

Poems of Carmen de Gasztold, collected and translated by Rumer Godden in *Prayers from the Ark and The Creatures' Choir* (Penguin Books, 1977), pray and sing from the perspective of various animals, stimulating my own poems.

Here's a cinquain I wrote after a morning walk at Greenbelt Lake:

> Heron,
> your wide-winged glide
> through fog to lake combines
> Samson's brash might with Simeon's
> blest hope.

Wise and loving Creator we praise You for Your creatures. Thank You for the way they teach us about You and about ourselves.

Making Soul Music

"My heart, O God, is steadfast; I will sing and make music with all my soul."

—Psalm 108:1

THE WORDS POEM and poet come from Greek words meaning make and maker. Psalmists, songwriters and poets make rhythmic word pictures to express otherwise inexpressible emotions of praise, joy, devotion and lament.

Reading Scripture's poems can shower us with the refreshing water of holy passion. But as we make our own God-directed poems, fountains spurt from our souls' reflecting pools. There are as many forms of poetry and song as there are people. Our poetry could be an improvised lullaby sung to a child; it could be a jazz solo or a liturgical dance.

Meditating on Scripture often stirs up our creative waters. Poet George Herbert (1593-1633) wrote the following sonnet to "The Holy Scriptures."

Oh Book! infinite sweetness! let my heart
    Suck every letter, and a honey gain,
    Precious for any grief in any part;
To clear the breast, to mollify all pain.
Thou art all health, health thriving till it make
    A full eternity: thou art a mass
    Of strange delights, where we may wish and take.
Ladies, look here; this is the thankful glass,
That mends the lookers' eyes; this is the well
    That washes what it shows. Who can endear
    Thy praise too much? thou art heaven's ledger here,
Working against the states of death and hell.
    Thou art joy's handsell: heaven lies flat in thee,
    Subject to every mounter's bended knee.

Lord, I want to make a joyful noise to You today. Please open my soul's fountainheads.

Making Everything Beautiful

Read Ecclesiastes 3:1-14.

> "He has made everything beautiful in its time. He has also set eternity in the human heart; yet no one can fathom what God has done from beginning to end."
>
> —Ecclesiastes 3:11

MOST OF ECCLESIASTES makes us uneasy. This one line testifying to God's making everything beautiful is overshadowed by hundreds that say everything is meaningless. Even this ray of beauty is dimmed by time constraints.

Yet God, the one who makes everything beautiful in its time, is not limited by time. And God has created us with an awareness of timeless beauty. Like trees, we are beautiful in different ways during different seasons of our lives. We don't need to use make-up or other means to make ourselves look younger than we are. By living fully, seeking and praising God in the stillness of the present moment, we can begin to see our Maker's eternal realm. There the one who "had no beauty or majesty to attract us" (Isaiah 53:2) becomes, in the words of a 17th century hymn, the "Beautiful Savior, King of Creation" (tran. Joseph A. Seiss, 1873).

In that beautiful kingdom of heaven there is a time to be born but not to die, a time to plant but not to uproot, a time to heal but not to kill, a time to build but not to tear down, a time to embrace and not to refrain, a time to search and never give up (because we will always find), a time to keep, not throw away, a time to love, not to hate, a time for peace, not for war. All who mourn will be comforted. God will "bestow on them a crown of beauty instead of ashes, the oil of joy instead of mourning, and a garment of praise instead of a spirit of despair" (Isaiah 61:3).

Thank You loving Creator for making everything beautiful in its time. Thank You for making us aware of the reality of Your timeless beauty, especially in Jesus, "the firstborn from the dead" (Revelation 1:5).

Making Every Effort

Read Luke 13:22 – 30.

> "Make every effort to enter through the narrow door...."
> —Luke 13:24

THIS IS THE only record we have of Jesus urging people to "make every effort." But in the epistles this encouragement or imperative is given at least six times. Peter, Paul and the writer of Hebrews cheer us on in our struggle to live in the reality of God's kingdom. They write to churches, knowing believers can never make it on their own: "Let us therefore make every effort to do what leads to peace and to mutual edification" (Romans 14:19—see also Ephesians 4:3 and Hebrews 12:14). Making every effort needs to be a team effort.

When Jesus, by his Spirit, saves us from whatever has been keeping us from the way of love, we enter his kingdom and join the struggle for peace and holiness. We try to follow Paul's advice: "work out your salvation with fear and trembling, for it is God who works in you to will and to act in order to fulfill his good purpose" (Philippians 2:12, 13). Making every effort can be difficult, unpopular and maybe even humiliating, but leads to the only true joy, peace and rest. Today, as in Jesus' day, empire-builders and money-making schemes open wide doors. But those who are first will be last and the last first.

Jesus, the door, thank You for opening the way to us. Holy Spirit, empower our efforts for the good of Your peaceable kingdom.

New Songs

Read Psalm 40.

> "He put a new song in my mouth, a hymn of praise to our God."
>
> —Psalm 40:3

WHAT MAKES A song new? A catchy tune? Compelling words? Imagination? Creativity? How could David keep writing and singing new songs?

Without God, "there is nothing new under the sun" (Ecclesiastes 1:9). We live, we die; we climb, we fall; we sing, we sigh. But God the Creator is also God the Sustainer and Renewer. When David was down, mired in a muddy pit he made for himself or struggling against mud-slingers, God kept renewing his heart and voice with new songs.

David's songs were not do-it-yourself ditties spouting pet peeves, touting ambitious schemes. Nor were they merely contemporary mood music. What made the Psalms new was their divine origin and audience. They were written under the influence of the Holy Spirit, who enabled the authors to see God's love, and therefore praise God, in all situations.

A great new song uplifts, sustains and lasts for generations. Thousands of years after they were written, hundreds of years after they were translated, Psalm lines still become new songs for new people every day. The psalmist summons everyone: "Sing to the Lord a new song" (Psalm 96:1). What is your new and renewing song?

Lord God, thank You for the Psalms. Let me hear and sing a new praise song to You this week.

New Mercies

Read Lamentations 3:19-26.

"…his compassions never fail. They are new every morning…."
—Lamentations 3:22-23

LIKE ONE HOUR of light in long dark Siberian winter days, this affirmation of God's renewing love shines forth in the prophet's long lament.

Newness, new life needs to be a daily thing. In a way we are all designed to be morning people. Sleep frees us to trust God's forgiveness, let go of striving and forget worries. We wake to a clean slate, a new day with the possibility of renewed openness to God's Spirit. Heart-to-heart time alone with Jesus sets the tone for the day.

Morning routines like centering, stretching, exercise, walking and journaling can unite body, mind, soul and spirit in prayer. These disciplines keep us faithful, reflecting God's faithfulness. Beginning each day in the same way helps me notice grace-filled nuances of God's newness. It could be a subtle change in weather or light; sometimes it's the surprising resolution of a conflict or problem; other times a recalled hymn line or Scripture verse prompts a new insight; often ideas sprout; always gratitude glows.

Lord God, we praise You for Your faithfulness. Open me to the wonder of Your love displayed in new ways each morning.

A New Spirit

"…pour new wine into new wineskins, and both are preserved."
—Matthew 9:17

NEW HOUSING DEVELOPMENTS, shopping centers and condos rose for miles around the small country church. Attendance dwindled. Midweek, then Sunday evening services were discontinued. Finally the pastor left, and the remaining faithful members, under financial and denominational constraints, closed the building.

Two years later, my husband and I were vacationing in the area of that small church. We found them on our denomination's website and decided to visit. On the outside, the small steepled structure still looked like a country church, out-of-place, nostalgic even, like a historical preservation. But the sign in front confirmed the website information. The church was alive and well—with a new name, rejuvenated in ministry with new and old members.

Joyful sounds of drums, guitars, piano, other instruments and voices greeted us and gave praise to the risen Christ. The pews and pulpit had been removed and a stage built on one side of the former sanctuary. On the other side and around to the front and back the congregation rose from semi-circles of chairs. Colorful banners and streamers hung from the ceiling.

Were these sights and sounds examples of Jesus' new wineskins? Not exactly. But they were vivid evidence of new life in people. The new wine is the Holy Spirit, and human hearts are the wineskins. God told his people: "I will give you a new heart and put a new spirit in you" (Ezekiel 36:26). God still pours out and preserves new wine. God still creates and preserves new wineskins with all kinds of amazing and lively results.

Renew Your churches, Lord. Renew us in heart and spirit. Keep us alive and growing, giving You all the praise.

Inner Renewal

"Though outwardly we are wasting away, yet inwardly we are being renewed day by day."

—2 Corinthians 4:16

IN OUR RETIREMENT and grand-parenting years, followers of Christ are getting newer, not older, by God's grace. Does anyone notice our newness? Are we busy with physical, social and financial concerns while neglecting the inside-out Holy Spirit power available to us each day?

In the power of the Holy Spirit, we can follow Paul's advice, "to put off your old self, which is being corrupted by its deceitful desires; to be made new in the attitude of your minds; and to put on the new self, created to be like God in true righteousness and holiness" (Ephesians 4:24).

God's inner renewal goes beyond vague feelings to transformation, re-creation. It's totally God's work, but we need to co-operate by tossing out old envies and greed, clearing away fearful, guilt-ridden or prideful clutter, resisting temptations to "conform to the pattern of this world" (Romans 12:2), and being open to God's new ways of renewing our minds. God's forgiveness enables us to forgive ourselves and others.

We may not launch a new non-profit or join the Peace Corps in our seventies (although some of us may). Our bodies or brains may give out, but God's regenerating renewal continues every day of our lives—and throughout eternity!

Keep me sensitive to Your renewal initiatives and directives today, Holy Spirit. Let people see on my face and by my life the newness You are working in me.

New People

Read 2 Corinthians 5:16-21.

> "Therefore, if anyone is in Christ, the new creation has come:
> The old has gone, the new is here!"
>
> —2 Corinthians 5:17

A GOVERNMENT LAWYER IN his mid-forties spends months in Brazil and returns recreated as a father, having adopted Luis, a young Brazilian boy. A young woman transplanted from Iowa welcomes a new member to our Washington DC congregation—an eighty-five-year-old widow whose only son died years ago—and begins calling her "grandma." Unlikely but solid, fruitful friendships, marriages and families are formed and reformed.

The possibilities are astounding! Christ's Spirit forges surprising new relationships among diverse believers at all stages of life.

How do we think of or view people? Paul calls us to let go of old stereotypes, divisions, judgments. When we see people, beginning with ourselves, from God's point of view, there is a new basis for reconciliation and friendship, compassion and commitment. "She's not a liar; she's my sister-in-Christ. He's not a felon or an addict; he's my brother-in-Christ. They're not aliens or welfare grabbers, they're our friends."

What a refreshing way to relate to people! How appealing this new life in Christ becomes!

Thank You Holy Spirit for correcting and clarifying our vision so that we see people in Your new, loving way.

New Names

Read Revelation 2:12-17.

> **"I will also give each of them a white stone with a new name written on it, known only to the one who receives it."**
> **—Revelation 2:17**

WHAT A FASCINATING promise! The context is Christ's letter to the church in first century Pergamum. We must not jump to the promises without heeding the warnings and conditions of fulfillment. But the Lord invites us as in the other letters: "Whoever has ears, let them hear what the Spirit says to the churches."

According to Revelation scholar, Darrell W. Johnson, there are at least nine good interpretations of this verse. According to the *NIV Study Bible* footnote: "Certain kinds of stones were used as tokens for various purposes. In the context of a Messianic banquet the white stone was probably for the purpose of admission."

Whatever the specific interpretation, the new name represents an ultimate status or identity, which is unique for each person. Only my Savior and Lord knows what role will suit me in eternity according to how he created me and what I did with the talents he entrusted me. When I read my new name engraved on that white stone, I will realize that it's perfect, that it's who I've always wanted to be, what I've always longed to do. How wonderful it will be to "know fully, even as I am fully known" (1 Corinthians 13:12)!

Keep me faithful and true to Your name, Lord Jesus. May I begin living up to the new name You will give me.

All New

Read Revelation 21:1-5.

"I am making everything new!"

—Revelation 21:5

CHURCH WAS THE nearest thing to heaven on earth for Minnie. But thrift stores were a close second. She loved to discover beautiful clothes which she combined and modified to create wonderful new outfits she could wear to church. Many of the thoughtful gifts she gave to friends and church family members were thrift store treasures.

It's hard to imagine "a new heaven and new earth," much less "the new Jerusalem, coming down out of heaven from God, prepared as a bride beautifully dressed for her husband." But we are all eager for "the old order of things" to pass away and for Jesus' rule of peace, joy, love and constant renewal to be fully revealed.

Wait a minute. Jesus says the old order of things *has* passed away, and I *am* making everything new. Yes, when Jesus defeated death and the devil by his resurrection, the old order of might-makes-right or money-is-power passed away. When the Holy Spirit came, Jesus began making everything new, starting with new people formed into a new body—the Church.

I can imagine Minnie collecting and sorting clothes for recycling from all over the world on the new earth. And she'll truly be in her element—church every day, home and church as one.

Lord, forgive our desires for new things and impatience with, or even resistance to, Your inward renewal.

Overcoming Doubt

Read Mark 9:14-29.

> "I do believe; help me overcome my unbelief!"
>
> **—Mark 9:24**

GOOD THING GOD doesn't keep score. If our belief / unbelief ratio had to be over 50 / 50 for God to pay attention to us, we would have no hope. Instead of measuring our belief level, Jesus helps us overcome our unbelief.

The man seeking release for his son may have come out of desperate hope and desire more than belief. His low-level belief may have dropped even lower after a crowd watched Jesus' disciples fail and the religious leaders started arguing. But when "all the people saw Jesus, they were overwhelmed with wonder and ran to greet him" (15).

In prayers for our children and grandson, I relate to the believing father seeking Jesus' help in overcoming our doubts about their spiritual health. In concerns for suffering children everywhere, I can identify with the disciples who could not drive out the evil spirit; I accept Jesus' counsel to pray and fast. In worship I pray to be overwhelmed with awe, eager to greet our Savior and Lord.

Lord Jesus, I do believe. In Your Spirit help me overcome the arguments and impotence of this unbelieving generation.

Overcoming Darkness

Read John 1:1-14.

> "The light shines in the darkness, and the darkness has not overcome it."
>
> —John 1:5

THE WORD "OVERCOME" is what my grandson would call "old-style." But it's a key word for delving into the mysteries of life and death, victory and defeat, power and weakness.

The prologue to John's gospel reaches back to the primordial triumph of light over darkness in creation. As God overcame the chaos of physical darkness throughout galactic reaches of outer space by creating light visible in sun, moon, stars and planets, so Jesus—the light of the world—overcomes the blindness and confusion of our inner space.

In the long light years before Jesus the Word came to live among us, it appeared that darkness would win out. David prayed: "Fear and trembling have beset me; horror has overwhelmed me" (Psalm 55:5). Jeremiah anguished about lying prophets and godless priests: "I am like a drunken man, like one overcome by wine, because of the Lord and his holy words" (Jeremiah 23:9).

In the centuries since Jesus defeated the devil and conquered death itself by his death and resurrection, popular powers of darkness in every generation again appear to gain the upper hand. Yet "the Light shines on in the darkness, for the darkness has never overpowered it—put it out, or has not absorbed it, has not appropriated it" (AB), cannot even comprehend or understand it, much less master it—"can never extinguish it" (LB). The light of life by the Holy Spirit of truth overcomes demons every day, not just symbolically on Christmas day.

Lord Jesus, permanent light of the world, we praise You. Thanks for overcoming all the shadows of fear, hate and falsehood.

Overcoming the World

"In this world you will have trouble. But take heart! I have overcome the world."

—John 16:33

TROUBLE IS A given. There will always be trouble-makers. People retaliate for troubles they have suffered and take advantage of others. Troubles, if not overcome by Jesus' power, harden into ideologies such as racism, materialism or even terrorism.

What troubles threaten to overcome us today? How can we "take heart"? Overcoming is not merely believing "deep in my heart" that right will prevail over wrong "some day" as the civil rights song proclaims. Jesus always is, was, and will be overcoming the world. The Savior speaks this bold, triumphant word of encouragement on the night of his betrayal, the eve of his crucifixion. Yet he uses the past tense: "I've conquered the world" (MSG). In the same way, John writes to believers years after Jesus' ascension: "You, dear children, are from God and have overcome them [spirits that do not acknowledge Jesus], because the one who is in you is greater than the one who is in the world" (1 John 4:4).

We who identify ourselves with Jesus, whose hearts draw sustenance and courage from Jesus' Spirit in us, also have overcome, can overcome, are overcoming, will overcome the trouble-producing world order.

Forgive our self-pity, Lord. We praise You for overcoming all troubles, even death itself.

Overcoming Evil

Read Romans 12:17-21.

"Do not be overcome by evil, but overcome evil with good."
—**Romans 12:17**

ANGRY COMPLAINING OR fearful worry are ways I begin to be overcome by evil. Most of the time it starts with something that's not evil. For example, after my daughter graduated from college she moved with her three-year-old son, whom I'd been caring for almost daily since birth, to Hawaii. Instead of rejoicing with her spirit of adventure and opportunity, I spiraled into bitter anxiety, self-righteous judgment and anger, all of which put greater distances between us than miles.

God's grace and mercy eventually pulled me out of that morass. The Holy Spirit drew me to discover cornucopias of goodness tumbling out of Scripture, nature, books and people around me. And the Spirit opened many overcoming ways for our family to stay in loving touch with letters, emails, phone calls and visits.

Paul's commands regarding evil, revenge and "your enemy" may strike us as extreme or irrelevant in our day. We may quickly assume they have nothing to do with nations or politics, only with personal relationships such as those between my daughter and me. Yet Paul is addressing Christians in Rome—an empire whose values were likely no less violent and vengeful than those of twenty-first century nations. As churches and citizens we can influence governments in ways that lead to peace rather than getting swept up in rebellious complaining, paranoia or militarism.

Deliver us from evil, Lord. Teach us creative ways to overcome evil with good.

Overcoming Satan

Read 1 John 2:12-14.

> "I write to you, young people, because you are strong, and the word of God lives in you, and you have overcome the evil one."
>
> —1 John 2:14

THE BAD NEWS is that the devil is still kicking. The good news is that Jesus is alive and active, daily renewing our strength to overcome the evil one. The aged apostle John compliments young or new Christians for bold vitality in victorious, Christ-driven living.

One strong way God's Word takes root and grows in us is through music. The worship songs we learn by heart sing out defeat to the devil. James Ward, on his 1998 CD *James Ward Live*, sings in the words of an unknown author: "Give Him praise all you people, give Him praise. Don't you know what praise is for?—it's an instrument of war! Give Him praise all you people, give him praise." One song reminds me of another. Lines from an old Sunday school song grab my attention today: "Mighty army of the young, lift your voice in cheerful song; send the welcome word along—Jesus lives! Wait not till the shadows lengthen, till you older grow; rally now and sing for Jesus, everywhere you go" (John R. Colgan, 1891).

The bad news is that the devil can turn youthful singers and spiritual overcomers into pharisaic imperialists and warmongers. But the good news rings out in verse two of another old favorite:

"Lead on, O King eternal, till sin's fierce war shall cease, and holiness shall whisper the sweet amen of peace. For not with swords' loud clashing or roll of stirring drums—with deeds of love and mercy the heavenly kingdom comes."

—Ernest W. Shurtleff, 1888

Overcoming by Faith

Read 1 John 5:1-12.

> "...everyone born of God overcomes the world. This is the victory that has overcome the world, even our faith. Who is it that overcomes the world? Only the one who believes that Jesus is the Son of God."
>
> —1 John 5:4-5

THE BUMPER STICKER said, "believe." It left me with questions: believe what, who, why? I had just read the chapter on Abraham, the father of believers, in Eugene Peterson's *The Jesus Way: a conversation on the ways that Jesus is the way*, in which he distinguishes between untested belief and true faith.

Belief expressed in that one-word slogan is a positive-thinking self-confidence. Its advocates preach creative visualization and conscious evolving. A second form of belief, sometimes overlapping with the first, is wishful thinking, desire or longing. Its practitioners say a lot of prayers. Finally, there is tested belief, the faith that overcomes the world, showing itself in loving, obedient action as well as prayer.

The apostle John uses a form of the word "overcome" repeatedly in his gospel, epistles and in Revelation. And he always points to Jesus as the power source for victory. This world-overcoming belief is not a self-generated determination. It is like the trust of a small child for a loving parent.

Spirit of God, we praise You for empowering us to overcome doubt as we believe in Jesus, realize our new birth, and live confidently in this faithless world.

Overcoming Together

Read Revelation 2:1-7.

> "To those who are victorious, I will give the right to eat from the tree of life, which is in the paradise of God."
> —Revelation 2:7

AFTER TWENTY YEARS of out-of-body experiences and mastering psychic, magical, meditative and astrological skills, Marcia thought she had mastered spirituality. But she was miserable, plagued with demonic visions. Finally she gave in to "an unexplained compulsion" to attend a church service. "In the opening minutes," she wrote, "I felt a love I had never known wash down over and through me, so powerfully that I started crying. I knew this love was from God, not from the music, the people, or the place." Marcia began reading the Bible and was fascinated with Jesus. I was greatly encouraged reading her story, printed out from cana.userworld.com and left on a rack in an Oregon health food store.

In letters to seven churches, Jesus, the supreme victor and life-giver, commends, chides and counsels believing communities on their progress in defeating evil forces such as heresy, complacency, lethargy and immorality. He concludes each letter with promises for those who "overcome" (NIV) or "conquer" (MSG) and the admonition: "Whoever has ears, let them hear what the Spirit says to the churches" (7).

Overcoming is not something we do on our own. We need Jesus. Where do we find him? In the Bible of course. But like Marcia most of us first experience the Holy Spirit of Christ alive in his body, the Church; he "walks among the seven golden lampstands" (1).

Thank You, Lord Jesus, for churches. Keep us faithful and discerning, always attentive to Your loving discipline.

Weeping Prayer

Read 1 Samuel 1:1 - 2:21.

> "In her deep anguish Hannah prayed to the Lord, weeping bitterly"
>
> —1 Samuel 1:10

GOD HEARS OUR tears. Tears in prayer reveal our sincerity and appeal to our Father's compassion. "The Spirit himself intercedes for us through wordless groans ...intercedes for God's people in accordance with the will of God" (Romans 8:26, 27).

Long before Hannah, God heard the sobbing, exiled Hagar and her dehydrated son Ishmael's cries. God's angel "called to Hagar from heaven, 'What is the matter, Hagar? Do not be afraid; God has heard the boy crying as he lies there.'" He told the weary mother to go on with her son and promised he would have many descendants. "God opened her eyes and she saw a well of water." And "God was with the boy as he grew up" (Genesis 21:15-20).

Provoked by her husband's other wife who had many children, Hannah "wept and would not eat" during the yearly religious festival (1:7). The priest assumed she was drunk: "Hannah was praying in her heart, and her lips were moving but her voice was not heard" (1:12).

Hannah went beyond tears in her prayer for a son. She made a vow to "give him to the Lord for all the days of his life" (1:11). The vow arose out of the tears—and out of God's loving response to the tears. When God blessed Hannah with Samuel a long prayer psalm poured out of her soul (2:1-10). When the boy was weaned she fulfilled her vow by bringing him to live in "the house of the Lord" with the priest (1:24-28). God continued to be "gracious to Hannah," blessing her with three more sons and two daughters (2:21). But it all started with bitter tears in God's house.

Thank You, Holy Spirit, for the gift of tears. Let them call us to prayer, knowing that You and Jesus intercede, and our loving Father sees and hears.

Answered Prayer

Read Psalm 65.

"You who answer prayer, to you all people will come."
—Psalm 65:2

EVERYONE PRAYS SOMETIME if only as a last resort, somehow if only with a curse. And everyone has the urge to praise and thank God, whether they recognize it or not. In David's words, "The whole earth is filled with awe at your wonders; where morning dawns, where evening fades, you call forth songs of joy" (8).

Thriller author and screenwriter, Andrew Klavan, was inspired by a character in a novel to offer a prayer of thanksgiving. Amazed at the joyful gratitude he felt over the next few days, Andrew continued to pray. Years later he testified in a magazine interview: "the work God did in my life was so profound and so exact and skillful in its surgery on those parts of me that were unhealed and broken and lost in the past, that I really would have had to stretch my analytical powers to have disproved what had happened to me" (*Radix:* 33:2).

Whether we have been praying all our lives or are just starting, Psalm 65 can wake us up to God-focused, praise-brimming, humble and communal devotion. We can make it personal by giving thanks for specific prayers answered, forgiveness granted, songs of joy called forth, wonders of God's creation commanding attention.

"You answer us with awesome and righteous deeds, God our Savior, the hope of all the ends of the earth and of the farthest sea…" (5). *When we were overwhelmed by sins you forgave our transgressions"* (3).

Regular Prayer

Read Daniel 6.

> **"Three times a day he got down on his knees and prayed, giving thanks to his God, just as he had done before."**
>
> —Daniel 6:10

DANIEL HAD ALL his bases covered. His future was secure—not because he "so distinguished himself among the administrators...by his exceptional qualities that the king planned to set him over the whole kingdom" (4)—but because he worshiped the King of kings.

Prayer is worship—an act of adoration, reverence or homage. Daniel worshiped God by kneeling before him. Prayer is also a way of life. Daniel prayed three times a day "just as he had always done" (MSG)—in spite of being framed by envious coworkers and officials, in spite of almost certain torture and death.

Prayer is both "giving thanks" and "asking God for help"—in that order (10, 11). Daniel praised the "God of heaven" who "changes times and seasons...deposes kings and raises up others" (Daniel 2:19, 21). Next, Daniel no doubt gave thanks for God's amazing provision in Babylon of health, wisdom, prosperity, success, even the lives of his friends preserved in a flaming furnace. Finally, Daniel laid his need out before God. I can hear him confessing his own fear of being thrown into the lion's den, praying for increased trust.

What personal prayer habits can we develop? I think of Muslims prostrating themselves at fixed times every day. I remember protesters being arrested for praying in the US Capitol.

Lord God, thank You for Daniel's faithful prayers. Thank You for rescuing and vindicating him. May my prayers be regular and full of gratitude.

Watchful Prayer

Read Matthew 26:36-46.

> "Watch and pray so that you will not fall into temptation. The spirit is willing, but the flesh is weak."
>
> —Matthew 26:41

READING GOD'S WORD can draw us to pray in new ways with each new approach, depending on our current life story and the Holy Spirit's leading.

In meditating on this Gethsemane prayer passage, Jesus' agony may move one to pray, "Father, please let it not be cancer; please may he stop drinking—yet not as I will, but as you will." Another time that same person or someone else may exclaim, "Thank You, Jesus, for going through with the sacrifice, being obedient to death, even death on a cross!"

Today our focus is on Jesus' command to his three closest friends and disciples. How he needed them to back him up in prayer, to stay awake, pay attention, and try to understand his agony! These same disciples had been "very sleepy" another time when Jesus took them "up onto a mountain to pray," but then "they became fully awake" and "saw his glory" (Luke 9:28-32).

Thank You Jesus for taking Peter, James and John with You. Forgive me for trying to face crises on my own, hiding my vulnerability, emphasizing Your praying in secret teaching over the one about two or three gathered in Your name. I confess my temptation to close my eyes to others' sufferings, to fall asleep rather than battle demons, to overeat and get complacent rather than fast, stay alert and pray. Keep me vigilant against temptation, Lord, and deliver us from evil. Thank You, Jesus, that You understand about my willing spirit and weak flesh. Thank You for forgiving and empowering Your weak disciples.

Night Prayers

Read Luke 6:12-15.

> **"Jesus went out to a mountainside to pray, and spent the night praying to God."**
>
> —Luke 6:12

A T GRANDMA'S FUNERAL dad told how she had taught him to pray, kneeling at her knee as she nursed his younger brother or sister. Sixty years later when she couldn't sleep at night she would pray for each of her six children and their spouses, each of her twenty-seven grandchildren, and each of her sixty-five great-grandchildren—each by name, prompted by photos, recalling needs and joys.

Each of us has our own prayer history. None of us is likely to pray alone outside all night like Jesus did the night before naming his disciples, and few of us have as large a family circle as my grandma's, but we can all aspire to the joys of more frequent and extended prayer times.

When I have a sleepless night hour, I like to put aside the pillow, but stay in bed lying flat on my back with my spine straight, breathing slowly. This is a very restful position preparing me for sleep, yet even with my eyes closed I am fully awake and present to God's Spirit.

A good bedtime prayer for adults is the one Jesus prayed as he died: "Father, into your hands I commit my spirit" (Luke 23:46). Then if we sleep and dream we trust the Holy Spirit to protect, refresh and illumine our minds. If we are wakeful we trust the same Spirit to guide us in praying for forgiveness, in giving thanks and in interceding for those whose names and faces God brings to our minds. And in the morning we give thanks for ideas given, decisions made, love renewed.

Lord Jesus, teach us to persevere and thrive in prayer.

All-occasion Prayers

Read Ephesians 6:10-18.

> "And pray in the Spirit on all occasions with all kinds of prayers and requests."
>
> —Ephesians 6:18

PRAYER IS A common theme in Paul's letters. Here the prayer directive climaxes the apostle's instructions on spiritual warfare: we need to don the full suit of spiritual armor from God, including "the shield of faith," in order to withstand evil forces.

God's Word is our sword, sharp and effective in the Spirit's power: "it penetrates even to dividing soul and spirit, joints and marrow; it judges the thoughts and attitudes of the heart" (Hebrews 4:12), preventing devilish accusations and deceit.

The devil wants us to believe that engaging in prayer and Bible study shows psychological weakness or immaturity. But, facing our fears, we admit that seeing ourselves as any more than needy children before God is dishonest.

Whenever I find myself boxing prayer away for special occasions, spending time with a child or even reading children's words brings me back to my child self in relating to God. I love being a foster grandma to Lily, in awe of rainbows, delighted with frogs, fearful of chainsaws and lawnmowers. I love reading Jen Lemen's columns in Faith@Work magazine giving her daughter Madeleine's fresh communion with God perspective. Two little books of *Children's Letters to God*, compiled by Eric Marshall and Stuart Hample (Essandess Special Edition, 1966 & 1967) ground me again in honest anytime prayer.

Father God, I want to pray like a child and like Your Son Jesus. Thank You for Your protection, and for the Bible and the Holy Spirit.

Effective Prayer

Read James 5:13-18.

"The prayer of a righteous person is powerful and effective."
—James 5:16

THE MOTTO ON grandma's old ceramic plaque proclaims "Prayer Changes Things." More importantly, prayer changes people, beginning with the person praying.

Depressed at home and stressed out at work, my friend Lori had been eating "badly" and not exercising. In exhausted desperation she slumped in her subway seat, unable even to nap. "God, help me," she prayed, and the floodgates of prayer opened. "It was selfish and whiny and gushing," Lori wrote. "It included all of the people and issues I've been meaning to pray for, everything that popped into my head." Afterward she felt much better in body and spirit, writing to her book group: "It gave me some perspective. I know it's not magic or anything, but it was just what I needed. I've been saving up a lot to say to God, because I was always too tired to pray."

But what about this "righteous" qualification of James? "There is no one righteous, not even one" (Romans 3:10). True, Elijah's prayers were powerful and effective; but "Elijah was a human being, even as we are" (17). He suffered from anxiety and depression after his publicly successful prayer for rain. It was only when he was at his wit's end, totally dependant on God, that he heard God's "gentle whisper" (1 Kings 19:3-18).

According to *The Student Bible Dictionary* (by Karen Dockrey, Johnnie and Phyllis Godwin, 2000), righteousness is rightness by God's standards, being right with God, living according to God's just and loving purposes—which is only possible because of Jesus, the Way. Therefore we pray, trusting in Jesus' name, for ourselves and others. "And the prayer offered in faith will make them well; the Lord will raise them up" (15).

Thank You Father God for forgiveness and righteousness in Christ Jesus. Thank You for Your abundant mercy and grace to all who call on You.

Led by Quiet Waters

Read Psalm 23.

> "...he leads me beside quiet waters, he refreshes my soul."
>
> —Psalm 23:2

WHERE ARE YOUR quiet waters? Mine are at Dayspring in Germantown, Maryland, where I go for monthly silent mini-retreats or quarterly Ember Days. After the opening gathering, I ask Jesus to lead me beside quiet waters and am drawn first to Alice's Pond, then Lake of the Saints, and finally Merton's Pond. All along the way the Lord my shepherd restores my soul as the Holy Spirit opens my eyes and ears to quiet surprises of waters, turtles, skies, breezes, trees, grasses, deer, flowers, butterflies and all kinds of birds.

An Internet search of "quiet waters" yields 249,000 web-pages. There are ministries, photos, paintings, poems and songs. There is a park in Florida with a notice stating, "bike trail closed indefinitely due to hurricane damage." There is a caravan park in England, a Lebanese restaurant in Australia, a book on Japanese psychotherapies, information for canoeists or sail-boaters, and even free desktop wallpaper—all linked with quiet waters.

But quiet waters are not always physical or searchable. The Good Shepherd leads grieving widows to refreshing quiet in crowded sanctuaries and empty bedrooms. He led the psalmist David to restoring quiet, not only as he cared for his sheep and when he looked for stones for his slingshot in preparation to face Goliath, but also inwardly after hurricanes like Saul's anger or his own grievous sins.

Lord Jesus, with You as my Shepherd I lack nothing. Thank You for leading me beside still waters.

Quieted and Contented

Read Psalm 131.

> "I have calmed myself and quieted my ambitions."
>
> —Psalm 131:2

IN THIS SMALL jewel of a psalm David talks himself into the proper frame of mind for worship and fellowship. It is a song of ascents, written to be sung as pilgrims made their way to God's temple in Jerusalem. Though David was, or would be, king of Israel, he knew that before God he was no better than anyone else. He compared himself to "a child of four or five who walks trustingly beside his mother" (NIV footnote).

Jesus, the King of kings, showed the same humble dependence on his Father. Throughout his earthly life, but notably when Satan tempted him to evade the cross and again in the garden of Gethsemane, Jesus stilled his natural human desires. Accused by Jewish leaders before Pilate, "he made no reply, not even to a single charge" (Matthew 27:14).

When his disciples asked, "Who...is the greatest in the kingdom of heaven?" Jesus brought a child into their circle. "Whoever takes a humble place—becoming like this child—is the greatest in the kingdom of heaven" he told them (Matthew 18:1-4).

How quiet is my soul as I pray or go to church? Is my heart proud like the Pharisee who prayed, "God, I thank you that I am not like other people" (Luke 18:11)? Is my mind noisy with "great matters or things too wonderful for me" (1) like the end times or judgment? Does my life pilgrimage encourage people to "hope in the Lord" (3) or in me and my church?

Loving God, keep me quietly content in Your tender love.

Quiet Wisdom

Read Ecclesiastes 9:13-18.

> **"The quiet words of the wise are more to be heeded than the shouts of a ruler of fools."**
>
> **—Ecclesiastes 9:17**

SOLOMON TELLS THE story of a poor man whose quiet, wise words saved a town besieged by "a powerful king;" but he "was treated with contempt and soon forgotten" (16 MSG). The jaded author of Ecclesiastes concludes that though "Wisdom is better than warheads, ...one hothead can ruin the good earth" (18 MSG).

The noise of conflict or foolish chatter overwhelms us at times. But another word of wisdom whispers: "Better a dry crust with peace and quiet than a house full of feasting, with strife" (Proverbs 17:1).

Author Kathleen Norris wisely offered her third grade writing classes the gift of quietness by urging them first to "make all the noise you can while sitting at your desk, using your mouth, hands, and feet." After only a few seconds of the din, they were glad to "make silence." The stillness became "a presence," which "liberated the imagination of so many children" (*Amazing Grace: A Vocabulary of Faith,* 1998). I join them in response to the One who says, "Be still, and know that I am God; I will be exalted among the nations, I will be exalted in the earth" (Psalm 46:10).

Almighty God, may we never act the fool, heeding the shouts of unwise rulers as if there is no God. Keep us from despair. May we rest and rejoice in Your quiet wisdom.

Quiet Strength

Read Isaiah 30:1-18.

> **"In repentance and rest is your salvation, in quietness and trust is your strength...."**
>
> —**Isaiah 30:15**

THE SOVEREIGN LORD, the Holy One of Israel, through Isaiah, pronounced words of woe to Judah for allying with Egypt, rejecting God's prophets, and basing their economy on oppression and deceit. Yet God never rejected his people. He kept offering true peace and quiet no matter the disastrous times, "but you would have none of it" (15).

Recognition of wrong-doing and weakness, leading to acceptance of total dependency on God, does not come easily. Yet this radically quiet stance is the only way to solid confidence. Like animals, our first instinct is to fight or flee. But unlike animals we have a third option—waiting for God.

Jeremiah advocates this patient attitude as well: "it is good to wait quietly for the salvation of the Lord." This prophet who was called by God while still in his teens prescribes what sounds like a disciplined exercise of quiet for young people: "It is good for people to bear the yoke while they are young. Let them sit alone in silence, for the Lord has laid it on them" (Lamentations 3:26-28).

Isaiah points to the time when "the Spirit is poured on us from on high" bringing God's fruitful justice and righteousness. "The fruit of that righteousness will be peace; its effect will be quietness and confidence forever" (Isaiah 32:15-17).

Lord God, quiet our self-justifications and self-help plans. Teach us Your fearless quiet.

not Quiet

Read Luke 19:28-44.

> "I tell you . . . if they keep quiet, the stones will cry out."
> —Luke 19:40

THERE IS "A time to be silent and a time to speak" (Ecclesiastes 3:7).Being quiet is good when we voluntarily and reverently quiet ourselves before God, but not when people try to silence those who are making joyful noises of praise to God.

To the Pharisees urging him to rebuke those who were honoring him as king, Jesus gave what turned out to be a warning. In a way, the stones did cry out as Jesus was killed: "The earth shook, the rocks split and the tombs broke open" (Matthew 27:51, 52). In a way, the rolled away stone cried out praise on the morning of Jesus' resurrection. And, in a way, Jesus predicted another stone-crying time when the Romans did "not leave one stone on another" (70 AD).

Confessing sin or speaking out against injustice are also times when it is wrong to be quiet and all the more wrong to silence others. David wrote, "When I kept silent, my bones wasted away through my groaning all day long" (Psalm 32:3). A Zimbabwean man told a reporter that, though he knew it was dangerous to be interviewed, he could not keep quiet about the desperation for food and water due to their dictator's regime.

Above all, in thanksgiving and praise we abandon all quiet. A grandmother in Zimbabwe, on receiving a bag of maize from the interviewer, sang and danced with her nine orphaned grandchildren in their one room house with a cross on the wall.

"You turned my wailing into dancing; you removed my sack-cloth and clothed me with joy, that my heart may sing your praises and not be silent" (Psalm 30:11, 12).

A Quiet Life

Read 1 Thessalonians 4:9-12.

> "...lead a quiet life...mind your own business and work with your hands...."
>
> —1 Thessalonians 4:11

PAUL ADVISES THE Thessalonian Christians to keep calm rather than getting carried away with the excitement of Jesus' imminent return. Later he appeals to those who "are idling their time away, minding everybody's business but their own...to work quietly for their living" (2 Thessalonians 3:11, 12). Paul himself earned his living as a tentmaker.

A quiet life is not an isolated life. Paul urges believers to love each other "more and more" (10). Nor is quiet living idleness that withdraws from the world in continual contemplation. It is not the notion of sinless unity with God or Buddhist Nirvana.

Quakers have been called "the quiet rebels." Their meetings are largely silent as each person looks inward, listening for a word from God. Yet they call each other Friends and have been known as hard workers, especially for the cause of justice. For example, in 1758 coming into Thomas Woodward's home for dinner, John Woolman questioned the status of servants he observed there. When told they were slaves, "he quietly got up and left the home without a word" ("The Social Justice Tradition" in *Streams of Living Water* by Richard Foster).

Lord Jesus, thank You for being a carpenter, showing us the value of working with our hands. Most of all, thank You for quietly submitting to death out of love for us. Show us ways to let our actions speak louder than our words.

A Quiet Spirit

Read 1 Peter 3:1-16.

"Your beauty…should be that of your inner self, the unfading beauty of a gentle and quiet spirit…."

—1 Peter 3:3-4

BECOMING A BEAUTIFUL, gentle person takes a lifetime of communion with God—for men and women, married or single.

My mother is a great-grandmother and I am a grandmother; we are both preachers' daughters, eldest daughters, who may well have become preachers ourselves if our denomination had approved it. We know our tendency to dominate or speak judgmentally, which turns the beauty of our laugh lines and smiling eye crinkles into mean frown creases, to say nothing of embarrassing our husbands or sons. Mom and I and others need to encourage each other to cultivate what Peter called the "incorruptible…charm of a gentle and peaceful spirit, which is not anxious or wrought up, but is very precious in the sight of God" (AB).

Gentleness is one of the fruits of the Spirit. Its root meaning is humility. The meaning of quiet in this verse is to be calm, settled and steadfast. Peter's epistle was written during a time when many women (and also slaves) were following the Way of Christ. Some women were abusing their new-found freedom; hence, Peter's instruction. It is still pertinent today. Strident arguments, as well as loud clothes and extravagant hairstyles, will detract from Jesus' beauty treatments in our personalities.

In our hearts, Christ Jesus, we revere You as Lord. May we always be prepared to give gentle, respectful answers to those who ask the reason for our hope (15).

Receiving a Spouse

"He who finds a wife finds what is good and receives favor from the Lord."

—Proverbs 18:22

MARRIAGE IS ONE of God's most wonderful gifts. How spouses receive this gift affects the health and longevity of their marriage.

Well-received marriages begin long before the wedding day or engagement. Especially while dating and even earlier, singles need to engage in prayerful searching, trusting Jesus' promise that those who ask from our Father in heaven will receive, those who seek God's good gifts will find them, and for those who knock doors will be opened (Matthew 7:7-11).

In receiving lines and at wedding or anniversary receptions, couples greet guests who bring congratulations and gifts. But the marriage reception is an everyday, lifelong, reverent and grateful acceptance of each other in God-given union.

Some Bible versions use the word "obtains," which connotes causing to come forth, drawing or bringing out. I guess it's not surprising that a man finding a "true" wife (AB) puts a smile on the face of the one who designed marriage in the first place. "Find a good spouse, you find a good life—and even more: the favor of God!" (MSG)

Thank You, Father God, for marriage. May we who are married continue to receive Your good favor, enjoying each other. May singles who are seeking Christian spouses look to You to open doors.

Receiving Jesus

Read John 1:1-16.

"Yet to all who did receive him, to those who believed in his name, he gave the right to become children of God."

—John 1:12

WHAT IF PRESIDENT Clinton or President Bush, wearing old, tattered clothes, moved into a homeless shelter or refugee camp? Would anyone recognize the former president? Would those who did welcome him? What if he stayed and promised those who trusted him whatever rights they needed: citizenship, pardon, property, even adoption!

Jesus was, is and always will be unimaginably greater than any president or king. He is God's son, God's creating word, God's life-light. Jesus is God, who "became flesh and blood, and moved into the neighborhood" (14 MSG).

Jesus' friend John wrote about his reception, how most people did not recognize or welcome him. They did not realize who Jesus was because they did not realize who they themselves were and how they needed him. "Yet"—thank God for that word "yet" at the beginning of verse twelve—many have, are and will perceive, believe and receive this one-of-a-kind neighbor warmly. They "believed he was who he claimed and would do what he said" (MSG).

We too believe. By God's Word and Spirit we receive Jesus. And Jesus gives us the privilege of being adopted into God's family, "made to be [our] true selves, [our] child-of-God selves" (MSG). And our receiving continues: "Out of his fullness we have all received grace in place of grace already given" (16).

Lord Jesus, thank You for coming to live among us. May we always recognize and receive You with humble, joyful gratitude.

Receiving the Holy Spirit

Read Acts 10.

> "They have received the Holy Spirit just as we have."
> —Acts 10:47

CORNELIUS THE CENTURION "gave generously to those in need and prayed to God regularly. He and all his family were devout and God-fearing" (2). He was "respected by all the Jewish people" (22). But only because an angel instructed him in a vision did Cornelius the Gentile contact Peter the Jew and gather his friends and family to hear the gospel. And only because God spoke to him in a solitary prayer-time vision and then directly by the Spirit—"Do not hesitate to go with them, for I have sent them" (20)—did Peter "and some of the believers from Joppa" (23) go to visit Cornelius in Caesarea.

Peter surprised even himself with the new not-for-Jews-only good news "that *everyone* who believes in [Jesus] receives forgiveness of sins" (43). As he spoke, "the Holy Spirit came on all who heard the message" (44). By the Spirit's power they received the word with joy, understood it, accepted it and began "speaking in tongues and praising God" (46). Peter realized, "They have received the Holy Spirit just as we have" (47). And he knew that the next step was baptism and full fellowship.

Are there people we avoid or exclude? Are we prejudiced against anyone—teenagers, hippies, ex-convicts, immigrants, bureaucrats, Muslims—because of self-righteous, judgmental stereotypes? Could any of them be "devout and God-fearing"—ready to receive God's Word and Spirit like Cornelius and his friends? Do the ways we praise God show that we ourselves have received the Holy Spirit?

Lord God our Savior, thank You for Your Holy Spirit freely given to all who will receive You in humble faith.

Receiving Each Other

Read Romans 16:1-16.

> "I ask you to receive her in the Lord in a way worthy of his people."
>
> —**Romans 16:2**

PAUL SENDS HIS letter to the Romans with Phoebe, a deacon from the church in Cenchreae. Before relaying personal greetings to about thirty individuals or households of believers in Rome, Paul commends Phoebe, who "has been the benefactor of many people, including me." He requests a well-deserved reception for her: "Be sure to welcome our friend Phoebe in the way of the Master, with all the generous hospitality we Christians are famous for" (MSG).

According to Paul, Jesus said, "It is more blessed to give than to receive" (Acts 20:35). Yet, as we see from Paul's note about Phoebe, receiving is linked to giving. And both are holy actions among people who may be strangers but who are brothers and sisters because of God's love in Jesus. "Freely you have received, freely give," Jesus told his disciples (Matthew 10:8).

A truly giving spirit is formed as we learn to receive humbly and gratefully, honoring those who give to us, as well as appreciating the gifts they bring. Monthly bulletin citations from our church council celebrate and praise God for the service of "church members who have blessed us or others in some special way." It's a good start. And I'm sure we can all find more personal ways to be good receivers of God's Phoebe-like servants and the gifts God brings us through them. We can begin by greeting each one by name, as Paul did.

Thank You, Jesus, for teaching us through Paul, Phoebe, and so many others who received Your Word and in living it out gave of themselves to others. May we too be generous receivers.

Receiving God's Word

Read 1 Corinthians 11:17-34.

> "For I received from the Lord what I also passed on to you...."
>
> —1 Corinthians 11:23

THE POWER OF the Holy Spirit transformed Paul into a living receptor and transmitter of God's Word. Probably one or more of the disciples who had been present at the Last Supper told Paul what Jesus said that night. But the Spirit etched Jesus' words on Paul's mind, enabling him to write almost exactly what the gospel writers wrote, quoting Jesus' words and instituting what we call Holy Communion (see Luke 22:17-20). Introducing the Spirit of truth, Jesus told his disciples, "the Spirit will receive from me what he will make known to you" (John 16:15).

Because of the Holy Spirit, this simple ceremony links Jesus' followers throughout the world, in all cultures, over 2,000 years. Rather than dying away as an old hand-me-down tradition, the Lord's Supper has flourished as a renewing "participation" in the body and blood of Jesus (1 Corinthians 10:16, 17).

How can we today make sure we do not partake of the Lord's Supper "in an unworthy manner ... without discerning the body of Christ" (27, 29)? I know my mind wanders too often, following my eyes, judging, envying and doubting rather than praising and loving. I need to cling to Jesus, our unseen host, by the power of the Holy Spirit. Sometimes closing my eyes helps. I pray with thanksgiving for those present and with longing for those absent. Sometimes the Spirit reminds me of a word from Jesus (John 14:26). Sometimes I need to open my eyes and see Christ's love reflected on the faces of those around me.

Lord, thank You for the living proclamation of Your sacrifice in Holy Communion. May we be live receivers and open conduits of Your Word and Spirit.

Receiving Life in Christ

Read Colossians 2:6-10.

> "So then, just as you received Christ Jesus as Lord, continue to live your lives in him…"
>
> —Colossians 2:6

PAUL URGES CHRISTIANS to stay refreshed, gratefully rejoicing, and receptive in the childlike mode of new believers. The soil of our lives must remain permeable to drink in God's Word and Spirit, allowing the taproot of our faith in Christ to grow ever larger, deeper, stronger. Seminary professor and preacher Barbara Brown Taylor wrote: "To follow Jesus means going beyond the limits of our own comfort and safety. It means receiving our lives as gifts instead of guarding them as possessions."

Following Jesus in that grateful way was a gradual process for me. I made public profession of faith and joined in celebration of the Lord's Supper at age seventeen. But not until age thirty did I realize the life-and-death urgency of my need to be mastered by Christ. And in each of the thirty years since I have needed to repent for relapses, those futile attempts at self-management. There are always clods to dig up, cultivation to be done in my heart-soil plot. Some people receive Christ more dramatically, as Paul did on the road to Damascus. But everyone is tempted to revert to pride, greed and other self-help ways of life.

Prayer is the great heart-soil tester. Do we quote verses like Mark 11:24—"Whatever you ask for in prayer, believe that you have received it, and it will be yours"—and forget that God knows our hearts? God sees the roots of our beliefs. "When you ask, you do not receive, because you ask with wrong motives, that you may spend what you get on your pleasures" (James 4:3).

Holy Spirit, how I need your cultivating and pruning to stay open to and growing in Christ!

Worthy to Receive

Read Revelation 5.

> "**Worthy is the Lamb, who was slain, to receive power and wealth and wisdom and strength and honor and glory and praise!**"
>
> —Revelation 5:12

THE WINDOWS OF John's Revelation open on millions of angels, and "every creature in Heaven and on earth, in underworld and sea, join in, all voices in all places" (13 MSG) bringing and singing their tributes. Like children displaying their artwork, singing, dancing, performing for their parents, we will all experience the joy of giving back and saying thank you.

Finally and forever giving and receiving will be perfect. No more frustrating failures to glorify God, to give Jesus the credit he deserves, to honor our Creator and Redeemer with full use of the talents and resources we constantly receive from the Holy Spirit. No more half-hearted giving to people or causes which may or may not serve well in building Christ's kingdom.

To ascribe worth is to worship, the ultimate, ecstatic, giving-receiving, blessing-blessed exchange. Our worship prefigures that heavenly scene, for we worship the one to whom "All authority in heaven and on earth has been given" (Matthew 28:18), the one to whom "the wealth on the seas will be brought" (Isaiah 60:5), the one "in whom are hidden all the treasures of wisdom" (Colossians 2:3).

Only Jesus could handle or manage power, wealth, wisdom, strength, honor, glory and praise. And he gave it all up to show us God's love. Prose fails me now; I long for that timeless perfection when Jesus will joyfully receive all our creative, passionate worship—whether in poetry, dance, music, visual arts or unimaginable and new combined voices.

Thank You Jesus! Please come soon. Sometimes we feel like we can't wait.

God's Shining

Read Psalm 80.

> "Restore us, O God; make your face shine on us, that we may
> be saved."
>
> —Psalm 80:3

ASAPH LEADS GOD'S people in a prayer song to their heavenly
Shepherd after Israel was ravaged by foreign invaders. Only
God, "enthroned between the cherubim," can rescue and restore
them. The song-leader prays that God will "shine forth," revealing his glory and power on their behalf. Three times the psalmist
appeals to the one who seems distant and aloof, first addressing
him as God, then "God of the angel armies, come back! Smile your
blessing smile: *That* will be our salvation" (MSG—3, 7, 19).

Today Christ's Church, rather than the nation of Israel or any
other nation, comprises God's people. Both worldwide and locally
the church has been ravaged. Like Israel and Judah, we pray for
an end to God's rebuke (16). We confess individual and corporate
responsibility. We pray for revival (18). Unlike most of God's Old
Testament people, we know we can never earn or deserve God's
smile. But neither can we live without it. And because God is love,
always gracious, merciful and compassionate, we never need to be
in the dark, feeling like God is angry at us.

God answered Asaph's prayer in Jesus, "the man at your right
hand, the son of man you raised up for yourself" (17). Through
Jesus, the light of the world, God's beaming smile goes beyond
blessing and encouragement to forgiveness and renewal.

*O God, thank You for Your ever, everywhere-shining, saving
love in Jesus!*

Shining Brighter

"The path of the righteous is like the morning sun, shining ever brighter till the full light of day."

—Proverbs 4:18

DAWN IS MY favorite time of day. Scanning the gradually visible, then brilliantly colored horizon, I try to guess exactly where the tip of the orange disc will appear. Clouds add wondrous hues and shapes to the mysterious panorama.

Sunset rather than sunrise is the usual metaphor for death. And too often we associate old age with decline or dimness instead of increasing brilliance. Yet the longer we take the Jesus' road, the better we see everything around us. This growing clarity of vision sharpens discernment and develops wisdom. The closer we get to meeting Jesus face-to-face, the more we bask in and reflect his light. This growing warmth mellows us and fires us up with ideas and energy for service during "retirement" years.

"The ways of right-living people glow with light; the longer they live, the brighter they shine" (MSG). History offers many shining examples, beginning with Abraham and Sarah in Genesis; most recently, I think of Billy and Ruth Graham and Jimmy and Rosalyn Carter.

> *Christ, whose glory fills the skies, Christ, the true and only Light,*
> *Sun of Righteousness, arise, triumph o'er the shades of night....*
> *Dark and cheerless is the morn unaccompanied by thee;*
> *joyless is the day's return till thy mercy's beams I see....*
> *Visit, then, this soul of mine, pierce the gloom of sin and grief;*
> *fill me, Radiancy divine, scatter all my unbelief;*
> *more and more thyself display, shining to the perfect day!*
> *—Charles Wesley, 1740*

Little Lights Shining

Read Matthew 5:1-16.

> "...let your light shine before others, that they may see your good deeds and glorify your Father in heaven."
>
> —Matthew 5:16

AS DALLAS WILLARD points out in *The Divine Conspiracy: Rediscovering our hidden life in God*, Jesus is talking to "common people, the multitudes," not the "best and brightest" by human standards. These are ordinary people going meekly about their daily lives—"poor in spirit," mourning, hungry for justice, thirsty for God's truth, persecuted but persevering. Jesus recognizes his lights of mercy and peacemaking in their transparent hearts. He tells them not to be shy because "You are the light of the world" (14).

Dutch painter Jan Vermeer was one of the first to portray ordinary people such as women, children and servants in homely workday settings. His canvasses are small, befitting the subjects, but an ethereal light emanates from the focal point of each scene, captivating our attention. Similarly God's Spirit of gentleness blesses and lights up the eyes, faces and hands of plain, down-to-earth people every day.

How does letting our light shine before others differ from doing "acts of righteousness in front of others, to be seen by them" (Matthew 6:1)? It's all in our attitude and motivation. Are we allowing Jesus' light to shine through us, acting out of compassion, common decency, even duty—or are we trying to show off, grab some glory for ourselves? Realizing we are all "little people" before God prevents our presuming we deserve credit. Jesus' encouraging word and people praising God keep us shining for him.

Dear Master, thank You for lighting up our lives and shining on others through us. Forgive us for acting like we are our own power-source.

Jesus' Shining

Read Matthew 17:1-8.

> "His face shone like the sun, and his clothes became as white as the light."
>
> —Matthew 17:2

TRANSFIGURATION IS NOT a familiar phenomenon to us. Only by this story of Jesus recorded in three gospels can we picture it. Like the word transformation, transfiguration comes from the Greek word meaning change or metamorphosis. Like the other miracles God worked through Jesus, the transfiguration was not a magic trick. Neither was it an ever-present halo or aura.

God, who is a Trinity, presents a triple revelation on this mountain: first, light radiating from Jesus' face and clothes; second, Moses and Elijah talking with Jesus. After these wonders Peter makes his brash building proposal and is silenced immediately by the third miracle. "While he was still speaking, a bright cloud covered them, and a voice from the cloud said, 'This is my Son, whom I love; with him I am well pleased. Listen to him!'(5)"

Come Be My Light, published after Mother Teresa's death reveals how after her initial ecstatic communications with Jesus, during the last fifty years of her life, all of the time she ministered in Calcutta, "she felt no presence of God whatsoever." Yet she was faithful in work and worship, "up at 4:30 every morning for Jesus, and still writing to him, 'Your happiness is all I want'" (*Time Magazine*, 8/23/07).

Like the apostle Peter and Mother Teresa, we may be blessed with transcendent or miraculous experiences. We can't stay on mountaintops, but we know from the lives of so-called saints and ordinary Christians that God shines through us, whether we "feel it" or not. We long for the holy city which "does not need the sun or the moon to shine on it, for the glory of God gives it light, and the Lamb is its lamp" (Revelation 21:23).

Shine, Jesus, shine! We praise You, and long for Your glorious return.

Shining Hearts and Minds

Read 2 Corinthians 4:1-7.

> "God, who said, 'Let light shine out of darkness,' made his light shine in our hearts to give us the light of the knowledge of God's glory displayed in the face of Christ."
>
> —2 Corinthians 4:6

PAUL WAS A leader—a church planter, preacher, scholar and writer. His authority came directly from Jesus, who spoke out of a blinding light and then through Ananias, and his power source was the Holy Spirit (Acts 9). Paul never takes credit for himself. He does not set himself up over other believers. He calls young Timothy "our brother" citing him as co-author of the letter (1:1), and he calls himself and Timothy "your servants for Jesus' sake" (5). Paul defends the gospel message. The message is what shines forth. The messengers are "jars of clay."

Who are church leaders throughout the world today? Has the Light of the world, the one who said, "Let there be light" shone in their hearts? Or has the god of this age blinded their minds, making them "stone-blind to the dayspring brightness of the Message that shines with Christ, who gives us the best picture of God we'll ever get" (MSG, 4)? Are we dazzled by their building complexes, shiny new cars, expensive clothes and brilliant rhetoric? Or does their simplicity and identification with lowly people keep our focus on Christ?

Many of us are called to lead in various ways. Like Paul may we remember that we are only clay pots, even risk being called crackpots, "to show that this all-surpassing power is from God and not from us" (7).

Holy Spirit, please guide and fill our leaders. May we never be blind to God's true light in Jesus.

Rising for the Shining

Read Ephesians 5:8-20.

> "Wake up, sleeper, rise from the dead, and Christ will shine on you."
>
> —Ephesians 5:14

PAUL QUOTES THIS line from an early Christian hymn, writing to new believers, who "were once darkness, but now…are light in the Lord" (8). He gently admonishes them not to lose their luster or get side-tracked into dark alleys.

Gail has been an alcoholic since her teen years. Now in her fifties, after abandoning her children, walking out of numerous AA meetings, churches, homeless shelters and detox programs, she is resigned to a dead-end existence, sleeping in a car with her drinking buddy.

It's easy for us who are sober to judge Gail harshly. We might assume that Paul's wake-up call applies to people like her and that she's failed to heed it one time too many.

But every church, even every Christian life, contains some sleeper cells. Alcohol is surely a mind-dulling, morals-destroying influence. But there are other, less obvious though no less deadly, "fruitless deeds of darkness" that need exposing.

Living as "children of light," we face our dark secrets, eager "to find out what pleases the Lord," to live wisely, seeking to "understand what the Lord's will is." Rather than falling asleep in church or being myopic and apathetic about mission, we "climb out of our coffins" (MSG), ready to rise and shine. Aroused by the Holy Spirit, we praise God and encourage one another with all kinds of hearty music.

Wake us up, Master. Use us to rouse others today.

Shining in the Dark

Read Philippians 2:12-18.

> "Then you will shine among them like stars in the sky as you hold firmly to the word of life"
>
> —Philippians 2:15-16

> Brightly beams our Father's mercy from His lighthouse evermore, But to us He gives the keeping of the lights along the shore.
> Let the lower lights be burning! Send a gleam across the wave.
>
> —Philip P. Bliss, 1871

AS A CHILD, this song along with "Jesus Bids Us Shine" (Susan B. Warner, 1868), "This Little Light of Mine" (Negro Spiritual), and "Brighten the Corner Where You Are" (Ina D. Ogdon, 1913) inspired me like Paul's star-shine promise. Even now I can more easily picture people as candles or lamps than as stars.

Being God's lights—"children of God without fault in a warped and crooked generation"—can be difficult and dangerous, like working with fire or electricity. Paul cautions: "work out your salvation with fear and trembling, for it is God who works in you..."(12, 13). Being beacons in a world of distortion and depression means avoiding "grumbling or arguing, so that you may become blameless and pure"(14, 15).

Paul poured out his life in sacrificial service but affirmed: "I am glad and rejoice with all of you"(17). There is great joy in seeing others discover Christ's life-light. And we look forward to joining the apostles, prophets, saints—all God's little and big lights: "Those who are wise will shine like the brightness of the heavens, and those who lead many to righteousness, like the stars for ever and ever" (Daniel 12:3).

Lord Jesus, give me oil in my lamp, keep me burning till Your new day dawns.

Trust in God

Read Psalm 20.

> "Some trust in chariots and some in horses, but we trust in the name of the Lord our God."
>
> —Psalm 20:7

IN TODAY'S PSALM David offers an invocation and profession of faith on behalf of the king's army before he leads them in battle. This trust echoes young David's answer to Goliath: "it is not by sword or spear that the Lord saves" (1 Samuel 17:45, 47). God had a long history of teaching his people where to put their trust.. Under Moses, Joshua, Gideon, and later Jehoshaphat, God dramatically demonstrated that no matter how his people are outnumbered, "the battle is not yours, but God's" (1 Chronicles 20:15).

To "trust in the name of the Lord our God" is to rely on, put our faith in, even "boast of" (AB) God's character. He is the "I AM"—the one who is always with us, always reliable, perfectly dependable, infinitely faithful. God is the only one fully deserving of our trust, no matter the "distress" we are in (1). He is the only one who can "grant all …requests" (5) and "make all …plans succeed" (4).

Printed on US coins is the motto, "In God we trust." Yet "the United States could earmark for defense as much as the next ten largest military powers combined and still reduce the Pentagon outlays by tens of billion dollars per year" (Bacevich: *The New American Militarism*, 2005). The problem with trusting in "chariots and horses" is you never know when you have enough.

Lord God of the angel armies, we praise Your holy name. We want to trust You fully. Forgive our misplaced trust. Please guide our leaders.

Trust for Life

Read Psalm 143.

> "Let the morning bring me word of your unfailing love, for I have put my trust in you. Show me the way I should go, for to you I entrust my life."
>
> —Psalm 143:8

THE EIGHT-YEAR-OLD SON of a single mom relayed a sober judgment: "My dad says you should never trust anyone but yourself." Sadly, that father repeatedly reinforced his own homegrown mistrust by canceling visits, contacting his son less frequently, failing to provide child support.

We trust as we love—people we love, people we know love us. The psalmist David loved God, knew God's love for him was "unfailing" and therefore put his full trust in God. Pursued by foes, faint of heart, not knowing which way to turn, David trusted God far more than any human being, including himself. David knew he needed "word" of God's steadfast love every day to activate his trust.

We need to hear God's "I love you" too. As we entrust our lives to our totally unconditionally loving parent God, as we trust in Jesus our ever-loyal friend, as we "meditate on all [his] works" (5), God's Spirit illumines this love. We realize ways we are protected, gifts of discernment, trustworthy people around us, dozens of ordinary but wondrous blessings, new possibilities for service.

"I spread out my hands to you; I thirst for you like a parched land. Teach me to do your will, for you are my God; may your good Spirit lead me on level ground" (6, 10).

All-out Trust

Read Proverbs 3:1-6.

> "Trust in the Lord with all your heart and lean not on your own understanding; in all your ways submit to him, and he will make your paths straight."
>
> —Proverbs 3:5-6

TRUST IN GOD is not simple for adults. What makes it difficult is not only that God is invisible, but that God's Word makes it an either/or, all-or-nothing, total-life engagement.

My trust in the Lord is half hearted or three quartered at best. Most of the time I rely at least partially on the sixty-plus years of understanding I've accumulated and sometimes on my gut feeling or impulse. But thanks be to God, all it takes is the desire to trust, plus acceptance that God knows best and that God cares most. God does the rest, flooding my heart with trust. And gradually that trust flows into my understanding, emotions, actions and directions.

Instead of hearing this proverb as an impossible imperative or confidence buster, I welcome its invitation to tune in ever more clearly to God's wisdom and love. As the old hymn puts it, "They who trust Him wholly find Him wholly true" (from "Like a River Glorious," Frances Ridley Havergal).

Lord God, thank You that in all things You work for our good. Thank You for calling us according to Your purpose. Forgive us when we act like we think we know more than You and then wondering why things aren't straightforward.

Blessed Trust

Read Jeremiah 17:5-11.

> **"Cursed are those who trust in mortals…. But blessed are those who trust in the Lord."**
>
> **—Jeremiah 17:5, 7**

GOD ALONE KNOWS who honestly puts their trust in him and who puts self-reliance or human agencies above him. God has ultimate authority to curse and bless people or nations. The curse goes back to humankind's first choice to trust themselves over God, and it extends to all of creation: "Cursed is the ground because of you" (Genesis 3:17).

Before God's people, the Israelites, entered the promised land, God made it clear that the land would be entrusted to them, not taken by their own strength or authority. As long as they trusted God their lives and the land would be blessed, but if they trusted in human powers, curses were bound to ensue. One way they were to show their trust in God was to let the land lie fallow for one year in every seven: "the land itself must observe a sabbath to the Lord" (Leviticus 25:2).

Like our first parents and like Judah in Jeremiah's time, our inclination is to "turn away from the Lord" (5) and trust in "development" or technology. Thank God for prophets who call us back from "the parched places of the desert" (6). Thank God for Target Earth International members who see God's creation as a sacred trust and purchase acres of rain forest in Belize for the Eden Conservancy. "They will be like a tree planted by the water that sends out its roots by the stream" (8).

Loving, all-powerful, all-wise Creator we trust You. Lord Jesus, we praise and thank You for redeeming us from the curse. Holy Spirit, keep us and our leaders trustworthy.

Protective Trust

Read Daniel 3 and 6.

> "…no wound was found on him, because he had trusted in his God."
>
> —Daniel 6:23

THE ROOT WORD for trust is related to an old French word, *triste*, meaning "place where one waits trustingly"—from which comes our word tryst. A blazing furnace and a lions' den are two of the most unlikely trysting places. Yet those are the very places where God's angel met four young Hebrew men who waited trustingly. "Shadrach, Meshach and Abednego came out of the fire" unharmed, "nor was a hair of their heads singed" (3:26, 27). Daniel emerged from his overnight with the lions, assuring the king: "My God sent his angel, and he shut the mouths of the lions. They have not hurt me, because I was found innocent in his sight" (6:22).

Where are our trysting places? True trust in God can't be confined to a place or time such as church on Sunday morning. In a society where most people trust in false gods of money and power, Christ-followers may end up in prison or another infernal situation. But "no wound" will be found on us. May we always be waiting trustingly, faithfully, fearlessly—knowing that God meets us wherever we are. Afterward we will join Daniel and his friends saying, "Surely this is our God; we trusted in him, and he saved us" (Isaiah 25:9).

> *"When I am afraid, I put my trust in You. In God, whose word I praise—in God I trust and am not afraid. What can mere mortals do to me?"* (Psalm 56:3,4)

Trustworthy - 1

Read Matthew 25:14-30 and Luke 16:10-12.

> "Whoever can be trusted with very little can also be trusted with much...."
>
> —Luke 16:10

PASTOR MORRIS RELATED Jesus' parable of the talents to his own trust growth. God first entrusted Morris with the gift of faith. As he exercised and invested this trust, it grew. He studied God's Word eagerly and spent many hours with other followers of Jesus. When the church needed a custodian, Morris was happy to volunteer. Soon he was leading a Bible study which grew in numbers. At the urging of his brothers and sisters-in-Christ, Morris attended seminary. Upon graduation he was ordained and has served as a hospital chaplain and congregational pastor ever since.

Morris was not over-confident or self-seeking. But neither did he hide his faith. The apostle Paul advises, "think of yourself with sober judgment, in accordance with the faith God has distributed to each of you" (Romans 12:3). Sober judgment is not the risk-avoiding fear of the man who buried his one bag of gold. Sober judgment is humble trust that God's Spirit has birthed faith in us for a purpose: "we are God's handiwork, created in Christ Jesus to do good works, which God has prepared in advance for us to do" (Ephesians 2:10).

What talents, funds, resources and people has God entrusted to me? Is my trust growing?

Thank You Father God for starting us off with as much faith as You know we can handle. Thank You for wonderful examples of and opportunities for spiritual growth.

Trustworthy - 2

Read 1 Corinthians 4:1-5.

> "...it is required that those who have been given a trust must prove faithful."
>
> —1 Corinthians 4:2

A TRUSTEE HOLDS legal title to property in order to administer it for a beneficiary. Paul identifies himself and Apollos as "servants of Christ ...entrusted with the mysteries God has revealed." They are trustees, not of a physical property, but of a priceless message—for an unlimited number of beneficiaries. The apostles prove themselves trustworthy as they faithfully serve the master by explaining the truths of the gospel to growing numbers of beneficiaries wherever they go. To another group of believers Paul wrote: "we speak as those approved by God to be entrusted with the gospel" (1 Thessalonians 2:4).

As beneficiaries today—receivers of "the mystery hidden for long ages past, but now revealed and made known through the prophetic writings" (Romans 16:25, 26)—we recognize that all the apostolic and missionary trustees were first beneficiaries themselves. At the same time we may realize that we are being designated as trustees for other beneficiaries—"in order that they may know the mystery of God, namely, Christ, in whom are hidden all the treasures of wisdom and knowledge" (Colossians 2:2, 3). The shift from beneficiary to trustee can occur swiftly and dramatically, as for a Muslim man in Guinea, West Africa, who saw a vision of Jesus. Or it may only be after years of receiving God's benefits that we begin to welcome opportunities for service as trustees in Jesus' worldwide kingdom.

Master, may we one day receive Your commendation: "Well done, good and faithful servant!"

Obey and Understand

Read Psalm 119:97-104.

> "I have more understanding than the elders, for I obey your precepts. I gain understanding from your precepts; therefore I hate every wrong path."
>
> —Psalm 119:100, 104

WE ELDERS CAN take a lesson from children and youths who learn by doing. And yet we reason that to say, "Just do it" is simplistic. There has to be a spark of motivation. For kids it may be love and respect for their parents or teachers. Ultimately for all of us God's law of love, revealed not only in the ten commandments but in all of Scripture, moves us.

Psalm 119 is the only psalm which was likely written before being spoken, written to be read silently and aloud, mulled over, reflected on, digested in prayer and put into action. The psalm teaches us how to approach and grow in understanding of God's Word.

Understanding, or standing under God's standard, comes in two intertwined ways: doing what God tells us and seeing the wisdom of God's instructions about life. Understanding is growth in the joyful adventure of glimpsing God, recognizing pure love and absolute truth, like a recurring aha moment. It's a heart thing, but it starts with our feet, hands, eyes, ears and mind.

Whenever I read or hear God's Word, I want to listen for a precept. As I do my housework, yard work, writing and care-giving, I want to rejoice in new understanding of God's precepts.

"I am Your servant; give me discernment that I may understand Your statutes" (Psalm 119:125).

Look, Listen and Understand

Read Proverbs 2:1-11.

"Then you will understand what is right and just and fair—every good path."

—Proverbs 2:9

YOU JUST DON'T understand!" the teenager whines when told he must be home by a certain time. Meanwhile the loving parent longs for the child to understand that the rules are for his own good. Yes, understanding is related to love. Francis of Assisi prayed: "O Master, grant that I may never seek so much to be...understood as to understand, to be loved as to love with all my soul."

The teacher of Proverbs urges his son, and so God urges us, along the bright way of understanding. The signposts are clear: listen—"turn your ear to wisdom" (2); take it to heart—"accept my words, store up my commands within you, apply your heart to understanding" (1, 2); pray—"call out for insight, cry aloud for understanding" (3); and seek—"look for it as for silver and search...as for hidden treasure" (4). Discoveries begin along the way: we "find the knowledge of God" (5); stand in awe—"understand the fear of the Lord" (5); receive wisdom (6, 10); enjoy knowledge "pleasant to your soul" (10); and God protects us (7, 8, 11, 12).

Job, of all people, felt misunderstood and cried aloud for understanding. Finally God spoke to him out of a storm, asking, "Where were you when I laid the earth's foundations? Tell me, if you understand" (Job 38:4). God went on and on with questions and illustrations from creation, and Job replied: "Surely I spoke of things I did not understand, things too wonderful for me to know" (Job 42:3).

Holy Spirit, as we meditate on Your Word may we be as eager to learn as You are to teach us.

Sing and Understand

Read Isaiah 40.

> "He will not grow tired or weary, and his understanding no one can fathom."
>
> —Isaiah 40:28

POET WILLIAM WORDSWORTH defined poetry as "thought too deep for tears." More recently, poet Galway Kinnell said "the secret title of every good poem might be Tenderness." Isaiah's message of comfort for God's people is one of Scripture's outstanding poems.

The prophet celebrates "the Sovereign Lord," the incomparably wise and powerful Creator, who, amazingly, is also the gentle shepherd. God is no ivory-tower intelligence alienating us by his vast knowledge; God's understanding is what we call empathy, compassion or just plain caring. In Jesus, God stands underneath with us supporting the weight of the world's woes. By the Holy Spirit in us, God enables us to walk, run and soar to new levels of understanding as we praise him in poetry and song.

> *Immortal, invisible, God only wise,*
> *in light inaccessible hid from our eyes,*
> *most blessed, most glorious, the Ancient of Days,*
> *almighty, victorious, your great name we praise.*
>
> *Unresting, unhasting, and silent as light,*
> *nor wanting, nor wasting, you rule day and night;*
> *your justice like mountains high soaring above,*
> *your clouds which are fountains of goodness and love.*
>
> —Walter Chalmers Smith, 1867

Give Thanks and Understand

"'Let not the wise boast of their wisdom or the strong boast of their strength or the rich boast of their riches, but let those who boast boast about this: that they understand and know me, that I am the Lord, who exercises kindness, justice and righteousness on earth, for in these I delight,' declares the Lord."
—Jeremiah 9:23-24

I HAVE AN eighty-four-year-old, lifelong-single friend whose name is Pauline Wisdom! She is humble, kind, understanding, unselfish, unassuming and always profoundly grateful. Like the firefly in a "Psalty" children's story and song, she "*glows*, and gives the glory all to God." In spite of many adversities, Pauline's life continues living up to the apostle Paul's quote of Jeremiah, "Let those who boast boast in the Lord" (1 Corinthians 1:31).

God knows our temptation to turn from celebration of his goodness to bragging about the gifts he gives us. He warns those who are outstanding—mentally, physically, financially—not to boast or glory in these blessings as if they are deserved.

Understanding is a gift that keeps us in our place. Through Jeremiah God promised: "I will give you shepherds after my heart, who will lead you with knowledge and understanding" (3:15). Understanding keeps us attentive, praising God for each ability, opportunity and leadership role we are given, for they are window-views of the Giver and doorways to sacred responsibility.

Gracious, wondrous, holy God, may I do justice, love mercy and walk humbly with You today (Micah 6:8). Give us leaders who glory in knowing You and show that they understand You by exercising kindness, justice and righteousness.

Read, Pray and Understand

Read Daniel 10:1-12.

> "Since the first day that you set your mind to gain understanding and to humble yourself before your God, your words were heard, and I have come in response to them."
>
> **—Daniel 10:12**

"A PPALLED" BY AN apocalyptic vision "beyond understanding," Daniel "lay exhausted for several days" (8:27). How then did he set his mind to gain understanding? First he "understood from the Scriptures, according to the word of the Lord given to Jeremiah the prophet, that the desolation of Jerusalem would last seventy years" (9:2). Next he "turned to the Lord God" in repentance and confession on behalf of "all Israel, both near and far, in all the countries where you have scattered us because of our unfaithfulness to you" (9:3-19).

Daniel could have rested on his laurels as a noble prince and dream interpreter, "in every matter of wisdom and understanding... ten times better than all the magicians and enchanters of Babylon" (1:20). But above all Daniel was a person of prayer. Baring his soul to God three times daily, Daniel realized his own sins and that all wisdom and goodness comes from God; he identified with God's people in exile rather than with the elite class he was privileged to join.

Are we struggling to understand cataclysmic visions of climate change, famine, war, AIDS or other disasters? Do we search the Scriptures and turn to God in repentance? "Knowing our own sin, we pray in solidarity with all other sinners.... St. Hermas, in his book *The Shepherd*, written about AD 140, writes, 'Repentance is great understanding'" (*The Illumined Heart: Capture the Vibrant Faith of Ancient Christians* by Frederica Mathewes-Green).

Lord have mercy! Holy Spirit, guide us to set our minds to gain understanding and humble ourselves before "the great and awesome God, who keeps his covenant of love with those who love him and keep his commandments" (9:4).

Understand with Jesus

Read Luke 24:13-49.

> "Then he opened their minds so they could understand the Scriptures."
>
> **—Luke 24:45**

UNDERSTANDING GOD'S WORD is spiritual tasting and digesting, not mental analysis and deconstruction. An elderly preacher munched on an apple as a distinguished theologian finished "proving that the resurrection of Jesus was false." During the question period, the seasoned believer asked the speaker whether the apple he'd eaten was bitter or sweet. "I cannot possibly answer that question, for I haven't tasted your apple," the scholar replied. "Neither have you tasted my Jesus," said the old man.

We get a clue to how Jesus opened the disciples' minds from his encounter with the Emmaus road travelers: "beginning with Moses and all the Prophets, he explained to them what was said in all the Scriptures concerning himself" (27). Yet "they were kept from recognizing him" (16) until Jesus "broke the bread" (35). Then, as our communion hymn says, they could "taste and see the goodness of the Lord." Jesus "disappeared from their sight" (31). But they recalled their "hearts burning within" (32) as Jesus opened the Scriptures to their understanding.

Open the eyes of our heart, Holy Spirit. May we taste and see You, Jesus, in all of Scripture.

Receive and Understand

Read 1 Corinthians 2.

> "We have not received the spirit of the world but the Spirit who is from God, that we may understand what God has freely given us."
>
> **—1 Corinthians 2:12**

ABRAHAM, A MUSLIM in Guinea, West Africa dreamed he was "entering a large building that looked like a cross." Inside he was "struck by the beauty of it and also by the exceedingly large number of people" there with him. I received this good news via email from the missionary to whom Abraham told his story.

Evelyn Underhill taught on the spiritual discipline of retreat: "We are going to be quiet with One who has everything to tell us and nothing to learn from us. The Holy Spirit educates us in inner stillness" (*The Ways of the Spirit*, 1990).

Whether on retreat, through a dream, or in prayerful Bible study, God's Spirit gets through to people. What God has freely given us is "Jesus Christ and him crucified" (2). This is the "mystery...that God destined for our glory before time began" (7). Anything else, including religious jargon or celebrity philosophies, is "human wisdom" (1, 5) from "the spirit of the world" (12), from "the rulers of this age, who are coming to nothing" (6).

Thank You Lord for Your messengers who explain "spiritual realities with Spirit-taught words." Guide us in discernment, Holy Spirit. Demonstrate anew Your power made perfect in weakness.

Life-giving Voice

Read Deuteronomy 30:11-20.

> "Now choose life, so that you and your children may live and that you may love the Lord your God, listen to his voice, and hold fast to him."
>
> —Deuteronomy 30:20

WANDERING IN THE wilderness for forty years, the Israelites were distracted by nostalgia for Egypt, jealousy or fear of other nations, and the temptation to worship gods they could manipulate. But some of them followed God's voice, spoken through Moses, to the promised land.

People don't automatically choose life at all costs. We fail to recognize that loving God, listening to God's voice, keeping close to God is the supreme life-generating choice. Or we forget that the choice to listen and follow needs to be made each day anew.

"Oh, God doesn't speak to us audibly like he did to Moses," someone says. The Israelites had a similar excuse: "Who will ascend into heaven to get it and proclaim it to us so we may obey it" (12)? God answers: "The word is right here and now—as near as the tongue in your mouth, as near as the heart in your chest. Just do it" (14 MSG)!

We are wired to be voice-activated by God's voice, the voice that spoke light and all life into being, the voice that spoke Scripture through Moses and many others. We have big advantages over the Israelites in Moses' time. God's voice became flesh, lived, died and rose again. And now that Jesus has ascended, the Holy Spirit voices God through all of Scriptures, through the communion of believers, into our hearts, mouths and lives.

Lord God, we do love You and trust You to show us the way of life today. Keep us listening to Your voice.

Glorious Voice

Read Psalm 29.

> "The voice of the Lord is powerful; the voice of the Lord is majestic."
>
> —Psalm 29:4

WHAT IF FORCES of nature had a life of their own? Suppose river cascades or ocean waves in willful pride swept over farms and cities. Or thunderheads and lightning conspired to boom and flash for hours every night without a drop of rain. What if tornados, volcanoes and earthquakes could decide for themselves where and when they would strike?

People who don't know the God of all creation fear and worship many human-projected gods. Baal was identified as the divine power present in thunderstorms.

Violent weather patterns are not gods, but sometimes God speaks through them, clearing the air, calling us to attention.

Seven times "the voice of the Lord" reverberates in David's hymn, calling hearers to cry, "Glory!" Thunder, lightning, wind and earthquake, as conduits of God's voice, shout the folly of nature worship.

Natural disasters remind us of God's power and majesty, not in fear, but in wonder and humility—and finally in grateful relief that God is *over* the flood waters, in charge of them. That voice spoke to Job out of a storm. And after "a great and powerful wind tore the mountains apart and shattered the rocks before the Lord," that voice came to Elijah as a "gentle whisper" (1 Kings 19:11, 12). His Majesty, the omnipotent king of the universe is as loving as he is powerful, always giving us strength and peace (11).

Lord God, who rides on the storm and makes winds Your messengers, we praise You. May we hear Your voice above all storms, physical and spiritual.

Guiding Voice

Read Isaiah 30:18-21.

"Whether you turn to the right or to the left, your ears will hear a voice behind you, saying, 'This is the way; walk in it.'"
—Isaiah 30:21

DRIVING IN A residential area, looking for a certain address, not focusing on the road, "Something told me to stop," said Mrs. T. She stopped and immediately saw and heard a young boy on a bike bump into the front of her car. With profound thanksgiving to God for preventing the child's certain injury or even death, she soon gave up driving. Years later at age eighty-seven, petite, alert, spry Mrs. T. walks daily—to the store, to the bus stop, or to Bible Study—praising God and looking for ways to serve people in need.

Through Isaiah, God warned "the obstinate children" who said to his prophets, "Tell us pleasant things, prophesy illusions… and stop confronting us with the Holy One of Israel!" (30:1, 10, 11). But God never gives up on his people. There is immediate grace and guidance for all who turn to the Lord.

> L i s – ten, listen, God is calling, through the Word inviting,
> offering forgiveness, c o m – fort and joy.
> Help us to be faithful, s t a n d – ing steadfast,
> Walking in your footsteps, l e d by your Word.

For my husband and I this week, the "voice behind" is Laremy and Becca's, singing this traditional Tanzanian hymn tune (translated by Howard S. Olson and arranged by C. Michael Hawn), pointing the Sunday morning crowd to Jesus, the Way. I rejoice hearing echoes of their guitar, drum and voices all week long.

Thank You Lord for voices that show us Your good ways. Holy Spirit, keep our hearts' ears open.

Get-ready Voice

Read Mark 1:1-8.

> "I will send my messenger ahead of you, who will prepare your way"—a voice of one calling in the wilderness, 'Prepare the way for the Lord, make straight paths for him.'"
>
> —Mark 1:2-3

ARE YOU READY?" I hear that question from various people each December. What they mean is "Got your tree up yet? Cards mailed?" And above all, "Shopping done?" I usually mumble something in reply, like "I don't do much."

But I want to say: all that Christmas hype is vanity and consumerism. I want to go back to the wilderness, away from the silver bells and the jingle bells, where I can hear John the Baptist and Isaiah's voices. I want to join with today's prophets getting ready for Jesus' return, preparing the way, making straight paths so that others will be ready to welcome the King.

"A voice says, 'Cry out.' And I said, 'What shall I cry? All people are like grass, and all human faithfulness is like the flowers of the field. The grass withers and the flowers fall, because the breath of the Lord blows on them. Surely the people are grass. The grass withers and the flowers fall, But the word of our God endures forever'" (Isaiah 40:6-8).

The gods of money and stuff have co-opted Christmas and Easter, turning them from holy feast days which follow the soul-searching fasts of Advent and Lent to frenzied holiday seasons. I thank God for prophetic voices like *Alternatives for Simple Living*, publishers of "Whose Birthday Is It, Anyway?"

Amen. Come, Lord Jesus (Revelation 22:20).

Good Shepherd Voice

Read John 10:1-30.

"...his sheep follow him because they know his voice."

—John 10:4

"They too will listen to my voice, and there shall be one flock and one shepherd."

—John 10:16

GRANDSON JUDAH FOLLOWS his mother's instructions for incoming calls when she's not home: he waits through the four rings and the recording inviting the caller to leave a message. "Hello, Judah?" I ask, and he picks up the phone immediately, recognizing my voice. If a stranger called or even someone who knew of Judah, but whom Judah did not know, he would not answer.

Jesus says he is the good shepherd and we are his sheep. He speaks to us heart to heart, Spirit to spirit, calling each of us by name. He guides and protects us. And he gives up his life that we "may have life, and have it to the full." Jesus makes clear that he has "other sheep" that he "must bring," as he prayed later "for those who will believe in me through their message, that all of them may be one..." (John 17:20-21).

How is the good shepherd calling me today? How am I hearing, recognizing and responding to him? In my rush to answer the phone—impulse to take charge, fix things, or talk to somebody—do I fail to hear Jesus' voice speaking to my heart?

Faith@Work is a quarterly magazine "empowering people to explore, discern and act on their many gifts and calls in the complexity of their daily lives for the good of God's world." Their theme for 2006 was "God's Call for You" and for 2007, "Sustaining Call." What a blessing to read stories of sheep from many "pens" who know and follow Jesus' voice!

Good Shepherd, we praise and thank You for the fully fulfilling life we have following You. Help us to trust Your voice to reach wanderers and those from other folds.

Praying Voice

Read Acts 4:1-31.

> "When they heard this, they raised their voices together in prayer to God."
>
> —Acts 4:24

HEARING THE CONGOLESE praying, most in French, some in heavenly tongues, seeing them scattered throughout our sanctuary on their knees, I recalled that first Jerusalem congregation.

"They lifted their voice to God with one accord" (KJV) after hearing Peter and John's testimony. In the same way, the individual voices of these immigrant believers rose "in a wonderful harmony in prayer" (MSG) after hearing the testimonies of several brothers and sisters in Christ. "They lifted their voices together with one united mind to God" (AB).

Another reminder of such a choir of prayers occurred at Grace Covenant Presbyterian Church in Blacksburg, Virginia on the evening of the day in April 2007, which began with thirty-three shooting deaths at Virginia Tech University. A few reporters were there, some with cameras, but soon left the kneeling duos, trios and quartets to their fervent outpourings of sorrow, compassion and trustful petition.

Whether we pray silently along with a pastor, take turns in praying aloud, or pray at home as couples and families, whether we participate in weekly prayer groups or attend a prayer concert in a time of tragedy or celebration, may we be "filled with the Holy Spirit" and speak God's word boldly like those early followers of Jesus.

Unite us in prayer, Lord. Thank You for songs of prayer and praise, which move us to a place of comfort and hope when we have had all we can take. "God of our weary years, God of our silent tears, Thou who hast brought us thus far on the way; Thou who hast by thy might led us into the light; keep us forever in the path, we pray" (African-American National Anthem, "Lift Every Voice and Sing" by James Weldon Johnson).

Commanding Voice

Read Revelation 1:4-20.

> "On the Lord's Day I was in the Spirit, and I heard behind me a loud voice like a trumpet, which said, 'Write on a scroll what you see....'"
>
> —Revelation 1:10-11

A S A WRITER I try to identify with John. I even envy him sometimes. Wouldn't it be wonderful to spend a Sunday in heightened spiritual awareness on a quiet island? John heard a clarion call which would shatter all writers' blocks; then he *saw* the divine speaker and many apocalyptic visions, as he was "carried away in the spirit" (17:3 and 21:10).

But the aged apostle was not enjoying an idyllic retreat. He was exiled to Patmos, outlawed as an insurgent for his witness to Christ. This self-described "disciple whom Jesus loved" was separated not only from his beloved Master who had ascended to heaven, but also from all the loving gatherings of Jesus' followers. Was he looking out to sea longing to hear hymns sung and words of peace spoken? Was he recalling that incredible resurrection day evening when "Jesus came and stood among them?"

The startling, commanding voice turned John around. The fearful vision stunned him to the ground "as though dead" (17). John writes that the Lord "pulled me upright, his voice reassured me" (17 MSG); Jesus identified himself and repeated: "Write...what you have seen" (19).

The more I write, the more I see writing as a gift, like reading, which everyone can enjoy, no matter how old or isolated or fearful we are. Hearing voices? Seeing visions? Engaging with God's Word? Use your voice to serve God as John did. Write it down for the churches (11).

Lord God, thank You for John's Revelation. Thank You for revealing Yourself to us through all of Scripture and creation, by the illumination of the Holy Spirit. Thank You for opportunities and calls to voice our testimonies in writing.

Designed for Work

Read Genesis 1:26 – 2:23.

"The Lord God took the man and put him in the Garden of Eden to work it and take care of it."

—Genesis 2:15

EDEN HAS COME to mean paradise, but paradise has come to mean a place of eternal leisure. We forget that Creator God created people to work, and work is a blessing.

After completing all of creation up through animals, God said, "Let us make human beings in our image, make them reflecting our nature so they can be responsible for …Earth itself, and every animal that moves on the face of Earth" (1:26 MSG). The detailed account of Adam's and Eve's creation begins before plants and rain, when "there was no one to work the ground" (2:5). God created us for the earth, even as he created the earth for us.

God does not take and put us in a garden workplace as he did Adam. But many jobs help keep our planet green. I was grateful when my husband was employed at NASA on the Tropical Rainfall Measuring Mission. Scientists still discover and name new plants, animals and stars. Artists express wondrous appreciation. God's good working purpose for us still holds. I believe people are most fulfilled in work that preserves, values and celebrates creation.

You bring darkness, it becomes night, and all the beasts of the forest prowl. The lions roar for their prey and seek their food from God. The sun rises, and they steal away; they return and lie down in their dens. Then people go out to their work, to their labor until evening. How many are your works, Lord! In wisdom you made them all; the earth is full of your creatures.
(Psalm 104:20-24)

Blessed for Work

Read Psalm 90.

> "May your deeds be shown to your servants, your splendor to their children. May the favor of the Lord our God rest on us; establish the work of our hands for us—yes, establish the work of our hands."
>
> —Psalm 90:16-17

MOSES' PRAYER THROBS with the longings of every old lover of God. We want to look back and see how God has worked for good in our lives. We want to look ahead and see our children and grandchildren praising God. Yet all of us, those starting out in a profession and forming families, as well those struggling to keep bearing fruit in old age, need to know our work is worthwhile, that we are making a lasting contribution. "And let the loveliness of our Lord, our God, rest on us, confirming the work that we do. Oh, yes. Affirm the work that we do! (MSG)"

This is my prayer inspired by Moses:

Lord God, thank You that my life is still a beautiful work in progress. Keep me active, serving and worshiping You, Master, with coworkers in Your kingdom, old and young. Thank You for my new work as a childcare grandma. Thank You for the call to write. Please follow with Your blessing so that people see the joyous light of Your love in all my work.

Honored for Work

Read Proverbs 31:10-31.

"Honor her for all that her hands have done, and let her works bring her praise at the city gates."

—Proverbs 31:31

THIS IDEAL WOMAN, "the wife of noble character," is known for five interrelated facets of work:

(1) Creative handwork (13, 21, 22, 24).
(2) Business management (14-16, 18, 24, 27).
(3) Physical vigor (15, 17-19).
(4) Planning and teaching (21, 25, 26).
(5) Charity (20).

Other words for noble are high-minded, virtuous and magnanimous. She "fears the Lord" and therefore is wise, faithful and praiseworthy. She is valued most by those who know her best, her husband and children. Her eulogist calls for official, public recognition of her excellent works. "She is the living embodiment of Woman Wisdom's teachings and attributes" (*The Women's Bible Commentary* chapter on Proverbs, Carol R. Fontaine).

I hear echoes of this tribute in the lives of some New Testament women such as Lydia, Priscilla and others whom Paul mentions. I see this Proverbs woman's energy, strength, dignity, prudence and generosity in many Christian women throughout history, right down to my two grandmothers, aunts and mother. I will not write off this poetic portrait as a superwoman fantasy.

Holy and loving God, thank You for creating us male and female, in Your image, capable of all kinds of good work. We praise You for the work of honorable women (and men). Forgive us when we "eat the bread of idleness" (27).

Day Work

Read John 9:1-5.

> **"As long as it is day, we must do the works of him who sent me."**
>
> **—John 9:4**

JESUS CAME AS a servant with work to do. Although Jesus was the all-powerful, eternal One, he subjected himself to working under the constraint of a deadline. Urged by his disciples to take time to eat when he was talking with the Samaritan woman, Jesus said, "My food is to do the will of him who sent me and to finish his work" (John 4:34).

The disciples didn't see the work, much less the deadline. They were busy looking for someone to blame for the man's blindness. Jesus redirected their focus and included the disciples in his mission: "we (*not only I*) must do the works of him who sent me." Working toward the deadline of the cross, Jesus was the lifeline to God's healing, saving, forgiving, illuminating love. Jesus also told his disciples: "you are the light of the world" (Matthew 5:14).

Lord Jesus, we praise You for Your labors of love on Earth, culminating in those hours of darkness, when You said, "It is finished." Father God, we praise You for raising Jesus to life, transforming the awful deadline to the awesome, eternal lifeline. Forgive our blindness to and judgment of needy people. Forgive our lack of urgency about the work you give us. Thank You for extending our deadline. We look forward to the eternal day beyond all deadlines.

Full-time Work

"Always give yourselves fully to the work of the Lord, because you know that your labor in the Lord is not in vain."
—1 Corinthians 15:58

IN 1886, AFTER "Thirteen Years Residence and Labor among the Lepers at Kalawao," Father Damien reported: "I am happy to say that my labors here, which seemed to be almost in vain at the beginning, have, thanks to a kind Providence, been greatly crowned with success." That year Joseph Dutton arrived—"a good companion for Damien, capable of laborious work." Both men died on that Hawaiian island and were lovingly laid to rest by the exiled people they served, Damien for sixteen years and Dutton for forty-four years. Their story is told by Sister Mary Augustine and Howard E. Crouch in *Two Josephs on Molokai* (Damien-Dutton Society, 1998).

Despair and death may be subtle influences where we work, not in our faces as for Damien and Dutton, the apostle Paul, Mother Theresa and others. But without Jesus' everlasting life-giving energy, guidance and blessing, our work is half-hearted and fruitless. In the words of an old song, we are "Workin' on a Building" for our Lord. Are there places where we can give ourselves more fully to that momentous work? Who are the people with whom we can be "always abounding in the work of the Lord" (rsv)?

Master, we praise You for the lives and work of those who have given themselves fully in Your service. We are confident that You, Holy Spirit, who began a good work in us will carry it on to completion. We continue to work out our salvation with fear and trembling, confident that You work in us to will and to act for the fulfillment of Your good purpose (Philippians 2:12-13).

Recreated for Work

Read Ephesians 2:1-10.

> "For we are God's handiwork, created in Christ Jesus to do good works, which God prepared in advance for us to do."
> —Ephesians 2:10

EACH OF US is a masterpiece, made in God's image. Our lives are works of art choreographed by the Master. Before creating the first human beings, God completed all the advance preparation for our good work of caring for planet earth and its creatures.

We are also God's children, dependent on God for wisdom, love and life itself. But like Eve and Adam we are duped by "the ruler of the kingdom of the air" (2) to think we know better. We want to figure out for ourselves what's good, which only leads to alienation from God, from each other and from creation.

Thank God for coming in Jesus, the only god-man, "who gave himself for us to redeem us from all wickedness and to purify for himself a people that are his very own, eager to do what is good" (Titus 2:14). We don't need to pile up random acts of kindness to feel good about ourselves, prove that we're good people and compete with other do-gooders. We are recreated in Christ Jesus "to devote ourselves to the good deeds for which God has designed us" (NEB).

Thank You, Father, for preparing works uniquely suited for each of us. We love You, Master, and want to serve You. Holy Spirit, please enable, inspire and guide us to do good works spontaneously and joyfully.

Work for the Master

Read Colossians 3:11 - 4:1.

> "Whatever you do, work at it with all your heart, as working for the Lord, not for human masters, since you know that you will receive an inheritance from the Lord as a reward."
>
> —Colossians 3:23-24

BECAUSE HIS LETTER would be read publicly in the Roman Empire, Paul did not endanger believers by advocating the abolition of slavery. "But for those who know the story, the clues are there…" as Brian J. Walsh and Sylvia C. Keesmaat explain in the "Ethic of Liberation" chapter of their book *Colossians Remixed: Subverting the Empire* (InterVarsity Press, 2004). The apostle has already stated the equality principle for God's new people: "Here there is no…slave or free, but Christ is all, and is in all" (3:11). Now he promises slaves an inheritance, making them not slaves but daughters and sons; plus he addresses not only slaves but masters, who "also have a Master in heaven" (4:1).

Paul's passion about work appeals to me. I want to love God with all my heart through whatever work I do—as Jesus did, no matter if he was teaching or washing his disciples' feet. I wonder about people who say about their job, "My heart isn't in it." If they feel robotic or resentful, is it time to look elsewhere for work? What if they are oppressed by human or inhuman, slave-driving masters? I long for everyone to have work they can do with intrinsic motivation, wholeheartedly for the Lord.

Master, may I work diligently on behalf of those whose work, bodies and lives are exploited. I remember You said, "whatever you did for one of the least of these brothers and sisters of mine, you did for me" (Matthew 25:40).

Exalted Leaders

Read Joshua 3.

> **"And the Lord said to Joshua, 'Today I will begin to exalt you in the eyes of all Israel, so they may know that I am with you as I was with Moses."**
>
> —Joshua 3:7

WHAT MADE JOSHUA a good leader? His name offers a clue. Originally it was Hoshea, a Hebrew name meaning salvation. It has since been changed to the familiar Joshua, meaning "the Lord saves" (the Hebrew version of the name Jesus). Joshua had forty years of on-the-job training with Moses, his mentor. He alone went up on the mountain as Moses' aide when God gave Moses the stone tablets of the law (Exodus 24:13). Caleb and Joshua's positive attitude about advancing into the promised land was based on their trust in God. When it was time for Moses to name his successor, God said: "Take Joshua...a man in whom is the spirit of leadership" (Numbers 27:18).

Joshua was a good leader because he was "the servant of the Lord" (Joshua 24:29). Trusting that the Jordan's flood stage upstream waters would stop flowing as the feet of the priests—who carried the ark of the covenant—touched the water, Joshua led the people across. "That day the Lord exalted Joshua in the sight of all Israel; and they stood in awe of him all the days of his life, just as they had stood in awe of Moses" (Joshua 4:14).

Who are our Joshuas today? Now that Jesus has come, does God still exalt spiritual and political servant leaders?

Lord God, open our eyes to discern the servant leaders You raise up in our day. Give us courage to follow them as they follow You.

Exalted Kingdom

Read 2 Samuel 5:6-12.

"And David knew that the Lord had established him as king over Israel and had exalted his kingdom for the sake of his people Israel."

—2 Samuel 5:12

RULE OF, BY, and for the people is complicated. Kingdom stories appeal to our longing for simplicity and stability. But democracies and monarchies alike have lapsed and collapsed under leaders who exalted themselves or their country over others. David was sinful, but he knew his place—under God and over the nation for the sake of God's people.

David's kingship previews the everlasting reign of Jesus Christ, under whom "God placed all things...and appointed him to be head over everything for the church..." (Ephesians 1:22). Messengers from Tyre brought supplies and workers to Jerusalem and built a palace for David, who "took this as a sign that God had confirmed him as king of Israel, giving his kingdom world prominence for the sake of Israel, his people" (MSG). Today God calls his worldwide kingdom "a royal priesthood, a holy nation" (1 Peter 2:9). We long to see all "the wealth of the nations" brought to "the City of the Lord" (Isaiah 60:5).

Jerusalem means "city of peace." In David's time the peace was hard-won and fragile. Jesus wept over Jerusalem as he rode into the city, crying: "If you, even you, had only known on this day what would bring you peace—but now it is hidden from your eyes" (Luke 19:42). Is peace still hidden? When will leaders and all people know Jesus, who already now reigns on David's throne? "Of the increase of his government and peace there will be no end" (Isaiah 9:7).

King of all kings, we exalt Your name. Let Your kingdom come on earth as in heaven.

Exalting God - 1

Read Psalm 57.

> "Be exalted, O God, above the heavens; let your glory be over all the earth."
>
> —Psalm 57:11

THE STORY BEHIND this Psalm begins with David and his men "far back" in a wilderness cave, on the run from King Saul and "3,000 able young men from all Israel." When Saul steps into the cave "to relieve himself" David's men urge David to kill him, but David spares Saul's life, "for he is the anointed of the Lord" (1 Samuel 24:1-7).

David crouches in the predawn hour, underground in a tunnel with his worst enemy blocking the only opening, and prays his way from fear to trust and praise. His confidence in God foretells the coming of Christ—"He sends from heaven and saves me"— and the pouring out of the Holy Spirit: "God sends forth his love and his faithfulness" (3). Twice David sings the refrain, eager to pick up his harp and lyre: "Be exalted, O God, above the heavens; let your glory be over all the earth" (5, 11). David addresses "God Most High…who vindicates me…rebuking those who hotly pursue me" (2-3). He leaves vengeance to God, not taking advantage of his enemy's vulnerability.

Lord God, may we, like David, be still and know that You are God. Yes, You will be exalted among the nations. You are exalted in all the earth. You, Lord Almighty, are with us; You are our fortress. (Psalm 46:10-11)

Exalting God – 2

Read Isaiah 2.

> **"The arrogance of all people will be brought low and human pride humbled; the Lord alone will be exalted in that day...."**
> **—Isaiah 2:17**

REPRESENTATIVES OF NATIONS, corporations, and even religions play "king of the mountain" like children. But the Lord has no need to shove, push and fight his way to the top. All nations will stream to his temple. He told his disciples: "I, when I am lifted up from the earth, will draw all people to myself" (John 12:32).

Isaiah predicts the ultimate Day of Judgment, which "the Lord Almighty has...in store for all the proud and lofty, for all that is exalted (and they will be humbled)" (12). The Lord's presence and "the splendor of his majesty" (10, 19, 21) will be awesome for those who "walk in the light of the Lord" (5), terrifying for the unforgiven who "hide in the ground" (19).

The business section of *The Washington Post* quoted the CEO of a Zurich-based yacht brokerage "on the difficulty of telling rich customers they have to wait four years for delivery of a super-yacht as demand soars for the hundred-foot vessels that cost nearly $10 million: 'Well, they're not the kind of people who are used to waiting.'"

We are shocked and offended by such idolatry. As in Isaiah's day, "there is no end to their treasures" (7). Yet the belligerent, "I'm better than you" spirit is not restricted to the wealthy. The words *arrogance* and *pride* are both derived "from verbs expressing 'height' and are ways in which we can think of ourselves 'more highly' than we ought to think (Romans 12:3)" (*Tyndale Old Testament Commentary, Isaiah*, J. Alec Motyer, IV Press, 1999).

Lord, teach us Your ways, so that we may walk in Your paths. You alone are worthy to be exalted. Prepare us for Your coming.

Humbled or Exalted

Read Luke 18:9-14.

> "For all those who exalt themselves will be humbled, and those who humble themselves will be exalted."
>
> —Luke 18:14

HUMILITY VS. EXALTATION is a major theme throughout Scripture. Ezekiel prophesied: "The lowly will be exalted and the exalted will be brought low" (Ezekiel 21:26). The apostle James put it this way: "Humble yourselves before the Lord, and he will lift you up" (James 4:10).

In the centuries following Jesus' ascension, the tax collector's simple prayer became known as "prayer of the heart" or "the Jesus prayer." It's length varies from "Lord, Jesus Christ, Son of God, have mercy on me, a sinner" to an urgent "Lord have mercy" or "Jesus, help!"

The Pharisee's so-called prayer could be blasphemy—using God's name vainly, as in "O my God, I can't believe how good I am and how bad everyone else is!"—or "Egad, the nerve of that greedy taxman to come in this holy place, especially with me !"

Our self-exalting is not as blatant. It may show in frequent use of "I," in avoidance of Jesus' name or the word sin, and in the use of abstractions, stereotypes and clichés. But without constant self-humbling, without awe for the holy Giver, our expressions of gratitude become self-congratulatory or condemning of others. Our petitions become judgments. Worst of all, we fail to hear God's answers as we tumble from our self-erected pedestals.

Lord God, thank You for opposing the proud but showing favor to the humble. May we submit ourselves to You. Thank You that when we stay low, coming near to You in Jesus, You come near to us and lift us up in Your grace, mercy and peace.

Christ Exalted - 1

Read Philippians 1:12-26.

> "**Christ will be exalted in my body, whether by life or by death.**"
>
> —Philippians 1:20

TENNESSEE SINGER-SONGWRITER James Ward paraphrased Paul's profession and composed his own beautiful piano accompaniment for it:

> For it is my deep desire / And my hope is eagerly
> That I not be put away to shame at all
> But that with perfect boldness / Just as I have been trying
>   to do
> So his honor may be seen in my body
> So his honor may remain in my body
> So his honor may be seen / If I live or if I die
> I may even have to die / So his honor may be seen in me
> For to me to live is Jesus Christ / And to die would be so
>   much better...

Paul's body is worn out and confined to prison. The obvious ending to his "I eagerly expect and hope..." is to be released, to be validated as a Roman citizen, and exonerated of all charges. But no, Paul is eager not to be ashamed, to hold his head high in courageous endurance "in chains for Christ" (13) to keep on preaching Christ joyfully and boldly.

As Jesus, the Word made flesh, is God incarnate, so his followers embody Christ. His life is magnified and exalted as we honor him in the whole of our bodily living—in what we eat and buy, in how we use our time, in our lifestyles and life paths—and also in how we die.

Lord Jesus, be glorified in my health, in my body, the temple of Your Spirit. Let me keep serving and praising You in all circumstances, for all the days You give me until that happy day I meet you in glory.

167

Christ Exalted - 2

Read Philippians 2:1-11.

> "Therefore God exalted him to the highest place...."
> —Philippians 2:9

WE NORTH AMERICAN Christians know humility is a virtue. We may even say or think we humble ourselves occasionally for prayer and worship. But humiliation? Never! However, Jesus fully and permanently humbled himself by becoming human. And in his love for us, in his obedience to the Father, who is Love (with whom he was equal and one), he was completely vulnerable and non-violent; he allowed himself to be tortured, publicly humiliated and murdered in the most excruciating way possible.

People who live in democracies are privileged. Christians living in democracies are highly privileged. Jesus "did not consider equality with God something to be used to his own advantage," but "set aside the privileges of deity" (6-7 MSG). Similarly, we should not use our privileged status to avoid or condemn others, but rather come out of our ivory towers, out of our comfortable or quibbling churches, going all out in loving our neighbors, pursuing peace and justice. We need to elect government leaders who do not exalt themselves or our nation or security or our "way of life" at the expense of the planet and the majority of people on it.

King Jesus, we praise You, longing for the day when every knee will bow to You. Forgive our failure to obey Your law of love. We confess our fears of suffering and humiliation.

Renewed Vigor of Youth

Read Psalm 103.

> "...your youth is renewed like the eagle's."
>
> —Psalm 103:5

IF EAGLES MAKE it through the first year and their habitat is safe with plentiful food, they live thirty–forty years, longer than most birds. They mate for life, return to the same lofty nest each year, expanding and rebuilding as needed, and they fiercely protect their young.

In old age David tells himself to praise God for youthful vitality. No matter what age we are, God revives us with new beginnings of gratitude, forgiveness, healing and rescue (2-4). In my faith tradition, Psalm 103 is often read at the Lord's table after sharing the symbols of his body and blood. With David we take stock of our souls and find them full of benefits. In the warmth of God's compassion, we bare our souls and feel them purified. All of us are children together in God's family, all young, full of possibility as we again receive a fresh start.

God is the eternal Father, the Ancient of Days: "you're always young in his presence" (MSG). He "satisfies your mouth [your necessity and desire at your personal age] with good; so that your youth, renewed, is like the eagle's [strong, overcoming, soaring]" (AB)! "Even youths grow tired and weary, and young men stumble and fall; but those who hope in the Lord will renew their strength. They will soar on wings like eagles..." (Isaiah 40:30-31).

Strong and loving God, we praise You for Your compassion and faithful care.

Tender Care of Youth

Read Isaiah 40:6-11.

> "He gathers the lambs in his arms and carries them close to his heart; he gently leads those that have young."
>
> —Isaiah 40:11

JESUS LOVES EVERYONE. There is no limit to his tenderness. He is the good shepherd who loves and cares for each sheep or lamb according to his or her needs. He knows that children, and all of us who are young at heart, rely on strong, tangible love to thrive. He knows that weary, young parents need gentle guidance and support. Isaiah's prophecy gives a small glimpse of Jesus who "took the children in his arms, placed his hands on them and blessed them" (Mark 10:16).

In his poem addressing a little lamb (1789), William Blake asked, "Dost thou know who made thee?" Like Isaiah, Blake shines a light on Jesus:

> He is called by thy name,
> For he calls himself a lamb.
> He is meek and he is mild,
> He became a little child,—
> I a child and thou a lamb,
> We are called by his name.

What an honor, what a comfort, what joy to be with children, as children in God's family like our brother Jesus. At church adults enjoy rocking babies, playing with toddlers, reading stories to pre-schoolers, singing and playing instruments with children of all ages. What a privilege for grandparents to offer counsel, encouragement and respite for harried young fathers or pregnant and nursing mothers.

Dear Jesus, teach us to tend Your lambs. Thank You for carrying us close to Your heart.

Good Young Days

Read Hosea 2:14-23.

"There she will respond as in the days of her youth."

—Hosea 2:15

GOD'S HUSBANDLY MESSAGE via Hosea promises a loving, forgiving, restoring fountain of youth to Israel, his wayward bride. She has only to follow him "into the wilderness" where he will "speak tenderly to her" (14). God will "remove the names of the Baals from her lips" (17).

Churches, like people and marriages, are usually most vibrant in their youth. How does the bride of Christ, his Church in its local manifestations, stay lively, fruitful, passionately devoted to her loving spouse? A city church creaks—not the building but the congregation's soul—and shrinks with age. Families move to the suburbs; young couples and singles choose new non-church lifestyles; prayer, Bible study, peace-making, care of the earth and the poor are neglected. A small-town or rural church dwindles as well. Youth migrate to cities; struggling families, immigrants, prisoners and children in need of mentoring or foster care are overlooked. Church becomes a superficial social or moral obligation.

Is God calling groups of his people out to the wilderness today—in retreat, in repentance for our prosperity and security worship which has ravaged the land and exploited the poor? Will we respond with youthful abandon, like the desert fathers and mothers of Christ's young Church? If so, God will surely renew us in spirit, in numbers, in diversity, in daughter churches.

Lord Jesus, loving husband of Your bride, the Church, keep us newlyweds forever! We long for the time when You will abolish bow and sword and battle from the land (18).

Youthful Vision for Mission

Read Joel 2:28-29.

"...your young men will see visions."

—Joel 2:28

PETER ANNOUNCED THE fulfillment of Joel's prophecy at Pentecost when God first poured out the Holy Spirit (Acts 2:15-21). Its fulfillment continues today as spiritual descendants of Joel and Peter speak and do God's Word with visionary vigor and stamina.

Young ministers and staff at New City Kids Church in Jersey City, New Jersey see a vision of "Loving Kids for Change—using the arts, learning and leading to disciple children into the whole life transformation of Christ." They see their mission clearly and state it on their website: "to follow a child in his or her development from age 6 to 19 and be the advocate, family, friend, counselor and Body of Christ to that child so that he or she is set on a path of life transformation that will carry him or her forward long after we are able to spend hours together every day."

On the national and international scale young and old, men and women follow Dr. Martin Luther King's dream. Thousands work in over hundred countries with organizations like Youth for Christ International, World Vision, and Youth with a Mission.

Pour out Your Spirit anew, Lord God. Speak Your Word of love and truth through our sons and daughters. Open our eyes and ears to Your visions.

Youthful Bravado

Read Mark 14:43-54.

> **"A young man, wearing nothing but a linen garment, was following Jesus. When they seized him, he fled naked, leaving his garment behind."**
>
> **—Mark 14:51**

BIBLE SCHOLARS HAVE guessed that this unnamed young man, mentioned only in Mark's gospel, could be Mark himself. The *NIV Study Bible* assumes the garment to be outerwear: "the absence of an undergarment suggests that he had dressed hastily to follow Jesus." The Message Bible offers another interpretation: "All he had on was a bedsheet."

Young people are known for being impulsive and in a hurry, also curious. What joyful smiles their stories bring! The young man's urgent venture to Gethsemane grabs our attention. We can identify with his panic on being grabbed in the dark by those "armed with swords and clubs, sent from the chief priests, the teachers of the law, and the elders" (43). They had already "seized Jesus and arrested him" (46). The young man was not alone in his fear of being associated with Jesus: "everyone deserted him and fled" (50). When Jesus was taken to the Sanhedrin, Mark's friend Peter "followed... at a distance, right into the courtyard of the high priest" (54). But when identified as a follower of Jesus three times, he denied it ever more vehemently.

Eager young followers of Jesus in Muslim countries today risk much to satisfy their curiosity. As with the young man of Mark's gospel, their curiosity is Holy Spirit fired. Christian peacemaking teams work in double jeopardy toward ceasefires and demilitarized zones—times and places where curiosity need not lead to panic.

Thank You Lord for those who escape and tell their stories. Thank You for welcoming us back when we desert or deny You.

Youthful Role Model

Read 1 Timothy 4.

> "Don't let anyone look down on you because you are young, but set an example for the believers...."
>
> —1 Timothy 4:12

PAUL ENCOURAGES THE young pastor, Timothy, his son in the faith. Denouncing "hypocritical liars" who "forbid people to marry and order them to abstain from certain foods," the apostle affirms the innate goodness of "everything God created" (2-4). He contrasts "godless myths and old wives' tales" with "the truths of the faith"—the living faith of Timothy's grandmother Lois and mother Eunice (2 Timothy 1:5).

Timothy was likely in his early thirties at the time of Paul's writing—the age Jesus was during his ministry. Today thirty begins the upper decade of youth, when we realize our need to stay fit through regular physical exercise. But, as Paul counseled Timothy, "a disciplined life in God is far more" useful, "making you fit both today and forever" (8 MSG).

The new name for our denomination's Young Calvinist Federation is Youth Unlimited. What an improvement! God forbid that we older people would "look down on" youth by trying to organize them as the lowest rung in a hierarchy of denominational agencies. Rather we rejoice in their exuberance and enthusiasm which is often unlimited by the prejudice and cynicism of adulthood. We welcome their honest expressions of doubt as well as faith, putting "our hope in the living God, who is the Savior of all people, and especially of those who believe" (10).

Father God, thank You for energetic youths who set examples for us "in speech, in conduct, in love, in faith and in purity" (12). May we always encourage them, loving them unconditionally.

Youthful Respect

Read 1 Peter 5:1-7.

"In the same way, you who are younger, submit yourselves to your elders."

—1 Peter 5:5

EVON PETER WAS twenty-three years old when he was elected Chief of the Gwich'in Nation in Arctic Village, Alaska. Never before had someone so young qualified for that leadership role. But he was a college graduate, familiar with government and computers. The Gwich'in people, facing the destruction of their caribou-based culture and habitat, knew they needed someone educated, who did not stay in the cities after graduation, but followed his heart back to Arctic Village. They trusted Evon Peter because he met with all of the former chiefs, receiving their counsel and endorsement. (I heard Evon's story on a film at the National Museum of the American Indian in Washington DC).

In contrast, young "King Rehoboam consulted the elders who had served his father Solomon," but rejected their advice, choosing to follow the advice of "the young men who had grown up with him"—also "the king did not listen to the people" (1 Kings 12:1-17). This resulted in the kingdom splitting and Rehoboam ruling only one or two of the twelve tribes.

The apostle Peter calls for balance between young and old, leaders and followers. Leaders are to be servants, "not lording it over those entrusted to you, but being examples to the flock" (3). Humility unites; pride divides: "all of you, leaders and followers alike, are to be down to earth with each other.... So be content with who you are, and don't put on airs" (5-6 MSG).

Thank You Lord for those who humble themselves under Your mighty hand. We trust You will lift them up in due time. Young and old, we cast all our anxiety on You because You care for us (7).

God's Zeal - 1

Read Numbers 25.

> "Since he was as zealous for my honor among them as I am, I did not put an end to them in my zeal."
>
> —Numbers 25:11

ZEAL FOR GOD'S honor is suspect in the twenty-first century. It's easy to label young Phinehas as a terrorist for his shocking stabbing of Zimri and Kozbi, in the act of intercourse (7-8). Self-important, cursory readers of Old Testament stories outside of their historic and cultural context can even view God, or the biblical writer's portrait of God, as the source of terrorism.

In comparison to a human being or even a super-power nation, God is the biggest, scariest entity there is, was or ever will be. If God had not spoken to us, revealing his true nature as love, he would be the sum of all our fears of the unknown and incontrollable. God is "jealous" and "punishing...to the third and fourth generation of those who hate me, but showing love to a thousand generations of those who love me and keep my commandments" (Exodus 20:5).

None of us love God purely or keep his commandments perfectly. A terrorist god would see us as merely numbers to be eliminated. But God, our loving Creator, sees individuals like Phinehas, who are zealous for his honor. God also sees people like "Zimri son of Salu, the leader of a Simeonite family" and "Kozbi daughter of Zur, a tribal chief of a Midianite family" (14-15). These two become scapegoats, and God restrains his anger.

Lord God open our eyes to ways we are being seduced into serving other gods, but may our zeal never victimize others. Thank You for Jesus, the ultimate scapegoat, who was zealous for your honor among us, so that you will never put an end to us in your zeal.

God's Zeal - 2

Read 2 Kings 19:20-37.

> "The zeal of the Lord Almighty will accomplish this."
> —2 Kings 19:31

ZEAL IS A God word. Enthusiasm, from the Greek *entheos* (inspired by God), is a synonym for zeal. Others are ardor, fervor and passion. One connotation I favor is eagerness: "The Lord is eager to cause this to happen" (*The Children's Living Bible*). Another is simply, profoundly, love: "My great love will make sure that happens. I rule over all" (*New International Reader's Version*). According to a Hebrew dictionary, "ardent zeal is a very strong emotion which desires some quality or possession of another—jealousy, in a negative sense, and zeal in a positive sense."

Through the prophet Isaiah, God assures King Hezekiah of his zeal against God-mockers and zeal for the "remnant of the house of Judah." Years before, during the reign of Hezekiah's grandfather Ahaz, Isaiah prophesied of the one from that remnant: "he will be called Wonderful Counselor, Mighty God, Everlasting Father, Prince of Peace. Of the increase of his government and peace there will be no end." At that time as well, Isaiah proclaimed, "The zeal of the Lord Almighty will accomplish this" (Isaiah 9:6-7).

Lord God Almighty, thank You for Your zealous protection, preservation and renewal of people devoted to You. We are eager with You for the accomplishment of Jesus' eternal reign of peace.

Zeal for God's House

Read Psalm 69.

> "I am a foreigner to my own family, a stranger to my own mother's children; for zeal for your house consumes me, and the insults of those who insult you fall on me."
>
> **—Psalm 69:9**

DAVID WAS "CRAZY for God"—in the words of Frank Schaeffer's new book title. Yes, he felt sorry for himself, but David confessed he deserved God's disciplining "wound" or "hurt." Crazy with consuming passion for God's honor, he cried out to God: "I love you more than I can say…. I'm madly in love with you" (MSG). David was concerned that others would be disgraced or shamed because of his guilt and God's punishment, and he was desperate for human comfort as he endured jibes from God-mockers. Centuries later, Jesus' disciples recalled David's passion when they saw Jesus go ballistic over those who were turning his "Father's house into a market" (John 2:13-17).

All of creation is God's house. His glory fills the earth. Carrie Barefoot Dickerson's zeal for God's creation consumed her with anger at the prospect of a nuclear power plant to be built near where she and her ancestors had lived and worked for generations. Carrie's hatred ate away at her health until, through daily prayer, she began treating adversaries "with kindness, respect, understanding—and even brotherly love." Nine years later Carrie and her group, Citizens' Action for Safe Energy, won their case against "the Nuclear Regulatory Commission, General Electric, the local power company, and the legislators seduced by their various lobbying organizations" (*Aunt Carrie's War Against Black Fox Nuclear Power Plant*, 1995).

Lord God, we praise You: Let heaven and earth praise You, the seas and all that move in them, for You will save Zion and those who love Your name will dwell there (34-36).

God's Zeal - 3

Read Isaiah 59.

> "he...wrapped himself in zeal as in a cloak."
>
> **—Isaiah 59:17**

WHAT A RELIEF to realize God's punishing zeal is like an article of clothing, not an aspect of his character! God's mercy and grace are intrinsic to his nature; his anger and retribution are necessitated by human injustice, violence and evil.

Like a loving parent, God weeps for the way our sins separate us from him. His face is hidden from us because we turn our backs on him. Like a wise teacher, God does not tolerate falsehood, foul speech or empty arguments. Like a good ruler, God keeps no company with those who do not value peace and justice.

God never stops speaking to us. "When I have spent my wrath on them," he says through another prophet, "they will know that I the Lord have spoken in my zeal" (Ezekiel 5:13). Jesus, God's promised liberator, will return "like a pent-up flood that the breath of the Lord drives along" (19). Meanwhile, God's Spirit is on us; God promises to breathe his holy Word in and through us, our children and their descendants always (21).

Lord, we look for light, but all is darkness; for brightness, but we walk in deep shadows. Like the blind we grope along the wall, feeling our way like people without eyes (9-10). Teach us Your way of peace and justice, truth and righteousness.

God's Zeal - 4

Read Ezekiel 39.

> "I will be zealous for my holy name."
>
> —Ezekiel 39:25

EUGENE PETERSON'S *MESSAGE* Bible's introduction to Ezekiel outlines the denial and despair responses of God's people to the catastrophic events of invasion and exile. The majority "refused to see what was right before their eyes (the denial crowd). There were also some who were unwilling to see anything other than what was right before their eyes (the despair crowd)."

But God gives amazing visions to Ezekiel—visions of God's zealous acts which rise far beyond catastrophe, even beyond the holy cleansing of apocalypse to wholeness and glory. Through Ezekiel God reveals links between his zeal and glory, between his glory in the temple and his zeal throughout the world, his glory and zeal displayed to Israel and to all people.

Reading Ezekiel today, we hear God's predictions of judgment: "In my zeal and fiery wrath I declare…there shall be a great earthquake in the land of Israel" (Ezekiel 38:19). God will pour out the full fury of his righteous indignation in "torrents of rain, hailstones and burning sulfur" (Ezekiel 38:22). For seven years (the number symbolic of completeness) weapons of war will be used for fuel (9). The chapter ends with God gathering his people, being "proved holy through them in the sight of many nations" (27).

Lord, You alone are God. Thank You that in Jesus You no longer hide Your face from us. Thank You for pouring out Your Holy Spirit on all people. May we too be zealous for Your holy name.

Zeal for Loving Service

Read Romans 12:9-21.

> "**Never be lacking in zeal, but keep your spiritual fervor, serving the Lord.**"
>
> —Romans 12:11

SOON AFTER HIS ninety-ninth birthday, Robert Jackson was honored as a "living legend" by *The Washington Post* for twelve years of four-day weeks "talking, singing and praying" at Waxter Children's Center, a Maryland state-run facility for juvenile offenders. Jackson's face in the news magazine photo is a study in compassion. The interviewer described his voice as sure and strong as he declared: "The ones that will listen, I tell 'em the right way to go. Above all, I tell them to go to church and Sunday school and to honor their mother and father." When asked about those who won't listen, Jackson said, "I can't help them, but I love them."

In today's Scripture, titled simply "Love" (NIV) or "Love in Action" (TNIV), Paul counsels: "Don't burn out; keep yourselves fueled and aflame. Be alert servants of the Master, cheerfully expectant" (MSG). The fires of our zeal must be the opposite of those that erupt from jealousy or revenge—as Paul makes clear in his quote from Deuteronomy: "'It is mine to avenge; I will repay,' says the Lord" (19).

Four times a year Dayspring Silent Retreat Center hosts Ember Day gatherings. During the six hour interludes, we focus on themes that link liturgical and natural seasons of the year. Alone in contemplation, together in devotion and reflection, we tend our spirit embers—"fan into flame the gift of God" (2 Timothy 1:6)—the zeal that is in us.

Holy Spirit, we praise You for the living, loving energy of people like Robert Jackson. Thank You also for opportunities for renewal at places like Dayspring.

Good Zeal

Read Galatians 4:8-20.

> "It is fine to be zealous, provided the purpose is good…."
> —Galatians 4:18

WHEN OUR PURPOSE is good, that is godly, God enables us to stick to that purpose and our zeal burns steady and bright. Sad to say, people with ungodly purpose can also be extremely zealous. Paul wrote about Israelites: "I can testify about them that they are zealous for God, but their zeal is not based on knowledge" (Romans 10:2). They trusted in themselves for goodness rather than in God through Jesus the Christ. Therefore the fire of their zeal was not of the Holy Spirit.

Paul warned Galatian Christians about the Judaizers: "Those people are zealous to win you over, but for no good. What they want is to alienate you from us, so that you may have zeal for them" (17). The apostle asked believers, "What has happened to all your joy?" (15).

Zeal, energy or passion for a project will fizzle if the purpose is self-promotion. God-generated zeal will not only withstand efforts to denigrate its holiness but will thrive in creativity, joy, peace and love.

I can testify that my writing progresses and is successful only as I am zealous to "know God" and be "known by God" (9). That is my prayer for each of you, dear readers.

Thank You Holy Spirit for good purpose. Purify and increase our zeal. Glory to God! Hallelujah! Amen.

Printed in the United States
137824LV00002B/1/P